FRANTIC 7

FRANTIC 7

The American Effort to Aid the Warsaw Uprising
and the Origins of the Cold War, 1944

JOHN RADZIŁOWSKI AND JERZY SZCZEŚNIAK

Translated by
PAWEŁ STYRNA

CASEMATE
Philadelphia & Oxford

Published in the United States of America and Great Britain in 2017 by
CASEMATE PUBLISHERS
1950 Lawrence Road, Havertown, PA 19083, USA
and
The Old Music Hall, 106–108 Cowley Road, Oxford OX4 1JE, UK

Copyright 2017 © Casemate Publishers, Jerzy Szcześniak and John Radziłowski

Hardcover Edition: ISBN 978-1-61200-560-7
Digital Edition: 978-1-61200-561-4 (epub)

A CIP record for this book is available from the British Library

Printed and bound in the United States of America

For a complete list of Casemate titles, please contact:

CASEMATE PUBLISHERS (US)
Telephone (610) 853-9131
Fax (610) 853-9146
Email: casemate@casematepublishers.com
www.casematepublishers.com

CASEMATE PUBLISHERS (UK)
Telephone (01865) 241249
Email: casemate-uk@casematepublishers.co.uk
www.casematepublishers.co.uk

Jerzy Szcześniak: For my father

John Radziłowski: For Radek and Diana,
my American children of Warsaw

Contents

Foreword to the Original Polish Edition

This book presents the story of the only daytime air expedition to provide assistance to the Poles during the Warsaw Uprising of 1944. It was the centerpiece of a United States Army Air Corps operation to deliver supplies to the Polish insurrectionists. The operation was part of a larger plan to conduct shuttle bombing missions that would originate in Western Europe, bomb targets in Nazi-held territory, land on Soviet bases, refuel, and then fly back on a second bombing mission to return to Western Europe. During Operation *Frantic 7*—conducted on September 18, 1944—American B-17 Flying Fortresses, supported by fighter planes, dropped arms, ammunition, medical supplies, and food over the city of Warsaw.

In a surprising way, this history wove itself into the fabric of my own life. While attempting to commemorate the death of eight American airmen in Dziekanów Leśny near Warsaw, my father awakened my interest in the fate of the American aircrews, as well as the desire to acquaint myself with their families, which inspired my decision to begin writing this book.

Initially, I wanted to only tell the story of one bomber and its crew, a Boeing B-17G "I'll Be Seeing You," commanded by Lt. Francis F. Akins, which crash-landed near Łomianki, Poland. However, research conducted over several years convinced me to broaden significantly the scope of the book. Thus, this work covers the fate of all the American pilots who perished during the September 1944 mission, with as much detail as possible.

While gathering and editing the materials constituting the basis of this book, I was deeply aware of the fact that, from the perspective of our times, this mission—one of many such operations during World War II—was but one episode in a much larger global conflict, whose role should not be exaggerated. The assistance brought by the Americans came too late and had no bearing on the dramatic situation of the Polish freedom fighters in Warsaw. During this time, spheres of influence in Europe had already been tentatively drawn and Poland consigned to Soviet control, leaving no place for a free, non-communist Poland. For many, this operation, conducted on the 49th day of the uprising, remains a mere gesture to placate Western public opinion, which had been moved by dramatic appeals for help from the Polish Government-in-Exile, the Polish community in the United States, and from Poland itself. Despite this, it is also important to remember that the events of September 18, 1944 have also been etched deeply into the memories of Varsovians. The brave demeanor of 1,220 young airmen, who risked their lives to carry out their duty, deserves our respect. This book was composed with them, as well as their families and friends, in mind.

Preface

On September 18, 1944 fires again burned throughout Poland's capital city of Warsaw. For 48 days, the armed citizens of Poland's Home Army resistance had battled the combined might of the Nazi Wehrmacht, Luftwaffe, and Waffen SS. Under orders from Adolf Hitler to exterminate the city's population and level its buildings, German forces aided by ex-Soviet auxiliaries had massacred 200,000 men, women, and children and turned much of the city—once dubbed the Paris of the East—into a smoking ruin. Yet the people of Warsaw continued to fight back from the rubble of their homes and workplaces. Armed with captured and homemade weapons, the Polish resistance had taken a fearful toll on the Nazi attackers, fighting house to house, room to room. But as the days of September passed, ammunition, food, and supplies dwindled.

Just a few miles east of the burning city, forces of the Soviet Red Army stood idle. Under orders from Soviet dictator Joseph Stalin, the communist legions, which had swept the Germans from much of east-central Europe throughout the summer months, waited as the Nazis destroyed the Polish capital. Once allied with Hitler, Stalin had entered the war only after Hitler betrayed their alliance and launched his forces against the Soviet Union in the summer of 1941. Stalin sought complete control over Poland. The existence of a large, independent, and anti-communist resistance movement in Poland was a major obstacle to that goal. Content to leave his former Nazi allies to destroy the Poles, Stalin waited and blocked aid for the beleaguered city and its people.

In London and Washington, Allied planners had tried for more than a month to arrange an airdrop to resupply the Poles. The Soviets had first refused to allow the flights, then, under pressure, slowly appeared to relent, playing for time as the Nazis pounded the Polish resistance in Warsaw day after day. Central to these inter-Allied disputes were a series of missions, codenamed *Frantic*, which had begun in June 1944. American aircraft from bases in England and Italy had flown over Nazi-held Europe, bombed targets, and flown on to an airbase near Poltava in Soviet-held Ukraine. Refueled and re-armed, the American planes flew back across Europe, bombed additional targets, and then flew home. Finally, after weeks of diplomatic back and forth, the Soviets agreed to the seventh and final *Frantic* mission.

Before dawn on September 18, 110 American B-17 Flying Fortresses rumbled off English runways loaded with supplies for the Polish resistance. Crewed by 10 men each, the heavy bombers assembled in formation under the watchful escort of 75 P-51 Mustang fighters, and began their flight across northern Europe, heading for the burning city of Warsaw.

Out of hundreds of battles fought by American forces in World War II and countless missions of the U.S. Army Air Corps, the *Frantic* 7 mission to Warsaw has been largely forgotten by most American historians. Its impact on the course of the war was negligible. Of the supplies it dropped, only a fraction reached the resistance fighters who needed them so desperately. The pilots and crew lost in the mission never became household names or featured in movies or documentaries about the war.

In Poland following the war, the country came under the control of a Soviet proxy regime that imposed a reign of terror on the country. The Independentist Home Army, which had fought the Nazis from the first day of the war, was treated as an enemy, its members persecuted, arrested, tortured, and often killed. The Warsaw Uprising was termed a "criminal" enterprise. American and Allied effort to help the insurgent fighters disappeared down the memory hole of official histories. Even after the death of Stalin, the *Frantic* 7 operation was ignored in favor of accounts that glorified Soviet and communist actions no matter how insignificant.

Yet, many Poles kept the true memory of the resistance to the Nazis alive, including the role played by the Americans. In the town of Łomianki outside Warsaw, the site where one of the mission's B-17s crashed after being shot down, local residents buried the remains of American airmen. After the war, the people of the small community tried repeatedly to raise a monument to the fallen airmen but were blocked by local communist party officials on the insistence of the government, which closely monitored the teaching, research, and commemoration of history. It was not until 1986 that a modest monument to the Americans was dedicated.

The story of *Frantic 7*, however, involves far more than a single air mission in a long and bloody war. The political wrangling over whether the mission would even take place and the subsequent collapse of the *Frantic* operations was a harbinger of the Cold War conflict between the Soviet Union and America and the Western democracies. Even today, the origins of the Cold War remain a subject with which historians struggle. In spite of the myriad revelations about the true nature of Soviet communism and the genocide and other crimes committed under the reign of Soviet dictator Joseph Stalin, many Western historians continue to treat Soviet actions during the war and its aftermath with nostalgia. Although recent studies such Anne Applebaum's *Iron Curtain: The Crushing of Eastern Europe, 1944–1956* have shown how the Cold War originated in Stalin's ambition and desire to dominate as much of Europe and Asia as possible, other historians continue to take an ambivalent or relativistic approach to the start of the Cold War. They treat it as the result of mutual misunderstandings, personality conflicts among the leaders of the wartime alliance, or as a kind of shared enterprise in which both sides were equally to blame.[1]

The political background to, and the fallout from, the *Frantic 7* mission clearly demonstrates that the Soviets were perfectly willing to allow the destruction of a major European capital and its 1 million inhabitants in order to further their desire for domination and control. Stalin cared nothing for the victims of Nazism or for the lives of the people of many nationalities who fought to defeat it. The war and its huge human and material losses were merely the means to an end for the communist regime.

The Americans and the other Western Allies came to realize this belatedly by the late 1940s, when the Soviets were already firmly in control of half of Europe and strongly vying for a commanding position in China and Korea. The chain of events that led to the recognition that the Soviets were an enemy in all but name began with the fallout from *Frantic 7* and the Warsaw Uprising.

Frantic 7: The American Effort to Aid the Warsaw Rising of 1944 is the result of a partnership between Polish writer Jerzy Szcześniak and American historian John Radziłowski. Szcześniak's original work *Frantic 7: Amerykańska wyprawa lotnicza z pomocą dla Powstania Warszawskiego* was the first book published in Poland on the *Frantic 7* operation and has been translated into English by Paweł Styrna and revised and supplemented for American readers by Dr. Radziłowski. Support for the project has been provided by the Columbia Heights-Łomianki Sister Cities Committee of Columbia Heights, Minnesota.

Frantic 7 is a work of scholarship meant to illuminate a forgotten but important corner of American and Polish history, but it is also a labor of love. The Sister City relationship between Columbia Heights and Łomianki, Poland, which gave birth to the book, was begun by residents of Columbia Heights, including the late Bernard Szymczak. His younger brother Walter (Władysław), the son of Polish immigrants, was the tail gunner on the B-17 "I'll Be Seeing You," and was shot down and killed over Łomianki. On the ground near Łomianki on September 18, 1944 was a young Pole who witnessed the fate of the stricken American plane and its crew. Ryszard Szcześniak's stories of that tragic day later inspired his son to begin the painstaking process of researching and reconstructing the details of what happened to the Americans and to chronicle their mission to Warsaw.

This book begins by examining the political and military situation in Poland and the uprising in Warsaw in 1944 that resulted. It then covers the origins of Operation *Frantic* and the critical political and military decisions that made *Frantic 7* such an important and controversial mission. It details the events of September 18, 1944 and the American effort to airdrop supplies to the Home Army in Warsaw. The book then turns to the fate of the Americans on board the ill-fated B-17 Flying Fortress, exploring all available evidence, and concludes by discussing the aftermath of the mission and its contribution to the worsening of relations between the Soviet Union and the Western Allies..

Acknowledgements

This book could not have been written without the assistance of numerous individuals, many of whom have already been mentioned throughout the work. They were willing to generously devote their time and knowledge to help. We are particularly indebted to Mr. Vincent J. Stefanek, without whose testimony many of the details regarding Lt. Akins' crew would have remained a mystery, as well as the late Prof. Paweł Wieczorkiewicz, who supported the project and offered valuable advice. We are also grateful to: Carolyn Beaubien, 390th Bomb Group Memorial Museum, Prima Air Museum, Tucson, Arizona; Jerzy Boć, Warsaw; Klemens Bogurat, Dziekanów Polski; Bogdan Chojnacki, Kątne; Francis R. Clark, USA; Prof. Janusz Durko, Museum of the Capital City of Warsaw; Edward Figauzer, Warsaw; Steve Gotts, 361st Fighter Group; Jan Kreusch, The Archive of Underground Poland: 1939–1956, Warsaw; Franciszka Kłódkiewicz, Kiełpin; Elżbieta Królak, Łomianki; Andrzej Kunert, The Archive of Underground Poland: 1939–1956, Warsaw; Norman Malayney, 25th Bomb Group, Pittsburgh; Milan Moravec, Prague, Czech Republic; Stanisław Pasternak, Dziekanów Polski; Peter Randall, Little Friends, UK; Garnett L. Akins Rainey, USA; Fred Sachs, 390th Bomb Group Memorial Museum, Prima Air Museum, Tucson, Arizona; A. Berkley Sanborn, USA; Jerzy Sienkiewicz, Warsaw; Stefan Szcześniak, Kiełpin; Chairman Krzysztof Stoliński, The Study of Underground Poland, London; Andrzej Suchcitz, The Polish Institute and Gen. W. Sikorski Museum, London; Wojciech Szabłowski, Nasielsk;

Zygmunt Walkowski, Warsaw; Ryszard Wiśniewski, Stara Wrona; Ken Wells, UK.

We wish to thank Hania Kawenzowska and Monika Szewczyk for helping to translate German-language correspondence. Special thanks also to Andrzej Kurowski.

We also with to thank Mr. Pawel Styrna of Washington, D.C., who translated Jerzy Szczceśniak's original Polish writing into English. The Columbia Heights (Minnesota)–Łomianki Sister Cities organization also deserves special thanks for helping to bring this project together and for its generous assistance in supporting the translation. In particular we wish to thank Ms. Delores Strand, Mr. Gilbert Mroz, and Mr. Dan Schyma.

CHAPTER I

The Uprising

Since the beginning of the German occupation of Warsaw in October 1939, Nazi authorities imposed the most severe military occupation ever experienced by a modern city. German military and police rounded up prominent citizens and civic leaders and executed them en masse at places like Palmiry, just north of the city: doctors, lawyers, priests, government officials, teachers, professors, military veterans, scout leaders, business people, and athletes. The German objective was to eliminate Poland's leadership class and turn the rest of the population into slaves, with the eventual goal of eliminating Poles as an ethnic group.

Poland's Jewish minority, approximately 10% of the country but nearly 40% of Warsaw's population, faced the greatest threat. Under Nazi occupation, Warsaw's Jews would be progressively isolated into a ghetto and later destroyed through a combination of starvation, disease, random terror, and, beginning in 1942, transportation to extermination centers like Treblinka.

During this period, the fabric of the city was torn apart by the Germans. Jews were forcibly relocated into the Warsaw Ghetto, which was gradually encircled by a wall, while gentiles were driven out. Jews from areas outside Warsaw were then added to the ghetto, creating severe overcrowding. Meanwhile, the rest of the population was subject to severe repression. Germans randomly closed off streets and rounded up everyone, deporting them to concentration camps or to be used for slave labor. Refugees from other parts of Poland flooded into the city, further straining already damaged social networks. German authorities imposed food rationing. Poles were allowed barely enough calories to live, Jews even less. Acts of defiance were subject to severe retaliation, and public executions occurred weekly if not daily.

Throughout this occupation and despite the extreme danger to anyone caught resisting Nazi authority, the Poles had built up a secret army of citizen-soldiers and an underground support network that functioned like a shadow government. Known as the Armia Krajowa (AK) or Home Army, it soon became the most extensive underground movement in the whole of occupied Europe. By the end of the war, AK brought together all ends of the political spectrum in Poland, except for the small communist party, which supported Stalin's effort to turn Poland into a Soviet colony, and a small rightist faction. The AK acted as the representative of the legitimate government of the country and worked in concert with the Polish government and armed forces in exile in London which sought to rebuild a free Poland after the war.

The goal of the AK was to prepare for a national uprising against the Nazi occupiers while at the same time resisting Nazi rule, gathering supplies and intelligence on the enemy, and working to hasten Germany's defeat. Home Army saboteurs attacked German supply lines to the Eastern Front, destroying trains, bridges, factories, and warehouses and tying down hundreds of thousands of Nazi soldiers and police. Daring teams of young men and women assassinated collaborators and top Nazi officials, including the SS Commander of Warsaw who was shot dead yards from his heavily guarded office in broad daylight. Home Army operatives gathered vital intelligence on German troop movements as well as on top-secret weapons testing. In 1944, the AK captured a nearly complete V-2 missile, Hitler's most secret weapon, which was being tested in central Poland. The missile was taken apart—with detailed drawings made of every piece—and secretly airlifted to Britain along with samples of the rocket's fuel. AK operatives documented Nazi efforts to exterminate the Jews, sending detailed reports and captured German documents on the atrocities by secret courier to London where they were shared with the Allies. (Sadly, the Allied leaders did little with the information.) Although little could be done to stop the Nazi machinery of death, a network known as Zegota was set up to assist Jews in hiding by providing money and false documents.

Throughout 1943 and early 1944, the AK waited and tried to harbor its strength while attempting to stay one step ahead of the Gestapo and the SS, which made constant efforts to infiltrate and destroy the Polish underground. By the end of 1943, the war had turned decisively against Hitler and his legions. The Allies had retaken North Africa, knocked Italy out of the war, defeated the German U-Boat campaign in the Atlantic, and begun daily bombing of major German cities. In the east, Soviet forces had inflicted a series of costly defeats on the Germans, driving them back toward the Polish border. By 1944 the Soviet juggernaut was pushing into eastern Poland.

Although the Poles welcomed each new Nazi setback, the looming presence of Soviet armies brought deep concern. In September 1939, the Soviets had allied with the Nazis to destroy independent Poland, with Stalin and Hitler dividing the country up between them. In the Soviet-controlled sphere of eastern Poland, Stalin unleashed his secret police, the NKVD, against the Poles. Between late 1939 and early 1941, tens of thousands were murdered and nearly 1.5 million people were deported to Soviet concentration camps in Siberia where many more died of hunger, disease, and overwork. From 1939 to the summer of 1941, Stalin supplied his Nazi allies with the oil and grain that allowed Germany to conquer much of Europe.

In June 1941, Hitler turned on Stalin and unleashed his forces on the Soviet Union. Stalin then became an ally of Great Britain and later of the United States and, by extension, of Poland as well. Stalin agreed to release the Poles he had held captive, and tens of thousands made their way to the British-controlled Middle East, among them thousands of former soldiers who quickly joined the ranks of the Polish army in exile. Nevertheless, it soon became clear that many Poles captured by the Soviets in 1939, particularly some 20,000 officers, had disappeared. Investigations into their whereabouts came to a dead end, with the Soviets insisting they knew nothing about the matter. In the spring of 1943, the Germans announced that they had found a mass grave at Katyń near Smolensk in Belarus containing the bodies of thousands of the missing Polish officers. Although the Soviets claimed the Germans had done the killing, it soon became obvious that the victims had been killed in 1940, well before the German invasion. Unfortunately, the British and Americans, to stay in Stalin's good graces, went along with Soviet propaganda despite the fact that their own intelligence services had confirmed Soviet guilt. The Polish government, however, supported an international Red Cross investigation as proposed by the Germans. Stalin used this as the pretext to break off relations with the Poles and form a puppet government drawn from a small coterie of Polish communists who had survived Stalin's own purges of the 1930s, liberally supplemented with Polish-speaking Soviet advisors. Poland's borders were shifted to conform to the new frontiers drawn by the Soviet dictator himself during the Tehran Conference in 1943. The Americans agreed to this arrangement but convinced Stalin to keep the details regarding Poland secret until after the 1944 presidential election in the U.S.A. Poland was to be governed by Polish-speaking communists from the so-called Union of Polish Patriots, followed by front groups known as the State National Council and the Polish Committee of National Liberation. This meant that Poland would be a Soviet-controlled entity with limited sovereignty.

Under Stalin's direction, the Soviets began to implement a plan to subjugate Poland to communist rule after the defeat of Germany. In the fall of 1943, Soviet partisans began a series of widespread attacks against the Polish underground and Polish partisans in eastern Poland. Polish underground leaders were invited by their Soviet counterparts to discuss cooperation against the Nazis, and when they showed up they were tortured and killed. Polish underground units were often betrayed to the Nazis or directly attacked by Soviet partisans. To counter this, the AK initiated Operation *Tempest*, ordered by the Commander-in-Chief, Gen. Kazimierz Sosnkowski.[1] The aim of Operation *Tempest* was not only to demonstrate the Polish will to fight the Germans, which the Soviets questioned as part of their international propaganda, but also to secure parts of Poland under Polish rule. The Poles also sought to actively underscore the Polishness of their eastern territories and the continuity of the legal government of the Polish Republic. One way to accomplish this was to bring the clandestine Polish armed forces, as well as the bodies of state administration and local self-government tied to Poland's legal Government-in-Exile, out into the open.

This situation was unacceptable to the Soviets, who cracked down mercilessly on every open manifestation of Polish sovereignty in areas vacated by Nazi forces. Their tactics followed a similar pattern in each region. Following a short period of frontline cooperation with the AK, in which the Poles assisted the Soviets in defeating the Nazis, the Soviets soon introduced repressive measures, often under the pretext of establishing the basis for future collaboration. Polish leaders were invited to "cooperation" meetings with Soviets and promptly arrested. Leaders were either killed or deported to the gulags of Siberia. Lower-ranking members were forcibly recruited into the Red Army or the auxiliary Polish communist army of Gen. Zygmunt Berling. The objective was to completely eliminate both the commanders and the rank-and-file members of the Polish pro-independence resistance movement.

The political pressure generated by these developments forced the AK to modify the goals of Operation *Tempest* in Warsaw itself. The Polish-based leaders associated with the Government-in-Exile hoped that a struggle in the heart of Poland, as opposed to the Eastern Borderlands which the West considered quite distant and exotic, would prevent Stalin from resorting to his usual methods. An uprising in the capital would allow the underground to demonstrate its own vision of a future Poland, thereby showing the world the aims of the Soviets toward Poland and the Home Army. In short, they would attempt to liberate the country through their own efforts.

The fatal flaw in this conception, from both a political and military perspective, soon manifested itself following the start of fighting in the capital. The city, located in the Red Army's theater of operations and also in the future Soviet sphere of influence, was left to its own devices by both the Soviets and the Western Allies.

On Tuesday, August 1, 1944, at 1700 h, an uprising broke out in Warsaw as a result of the growing expectations of the inevitable German defeat and the impending approach of the Red Army. For nearly five years the Varsovians had burned with desire to strike back at the Nazis.

Polish forces numbered close to 50,000, mostly members of the Home Army along with some smaller resistance groups mostly serving under Home Army command. Many of Home Army soldiers were young, including units made up of Boy Scouts and Girl Guides (the Polish equivalent of the Girl Scouts). Despite their numbers, they were poorly armed and only one in ten soldiers had a weapon at the start of the fighting. Weapons consisted of a mixture of prewar arms hidden during the occupation, German weapons captured or purchased on the black market, arms received in air drops from the West, and weapons made in secret workshops—including submachineguns, grenades, and even flamethrowers. They faced a huge array of German forces, including two SS battlegroups, the city's army garrison, the Hermann Göring Panzer division, and many support units including aircraft and heavy siege artillery.

In the first days of the fighting the Poles liberated much of the central area of Warsaw, including the Old Town and Central City districts. Yet, lacking heavy weapons, they were unable to capture the bridges over the Vistula and several key points within the city which had been heavily fortified by the Germans prior to the uprising. While defending the areas they had liberated, the Home Army then sought to eliminate the isolated Nazi positions. One of these positions was a small concentration camp set up in the ruins of the former Jewish ghetto. Officially called KL Warschau, the camp was heavily fortified and at the start of the uprising contained about 400 Jewish prisoners. On August 5, a volunteer detachment from AK's Battalion Zoska, led by Wacław Micuta, attacked the camp. Commanding a captured Panther tank, Micuta drove over the barricades around the camp, narrowly avoiding a cluster of German grenades. A single shot from the tank's main gun destroyed one of the watchtowers and Polish soldiers poured into the camp. Within a short time, the Nazi guards were dead or fleeing in panic. Reaching the inner courtyard of the camp, Micuta found an astonishing sight. Far from being broken by the brutality of their guards, over a hundred prisoners stood at attention. One of the men stepped forward and saluted. "Sergeant Henryk Lederman, sir," he reported, "and the Jewish Battalion ready for action." The Jewish volunteers were accepted under

Micuta's command, and, though many would die in fighting, he recalled them as "exceptionally brave, ingenious and faithful" soldiers.[2] Though it was small, it was the first Nazi camp with live prisoners liberated by Allied soldiers.

When news of the uprising reached Hitler, he went into a rage. He ordered the complete destruction of the city and the death of all its 1.2 million inhabitants. Heinrich Himmler, SS Reichsführer, was eager to comply. He confidently predicted, "Warsaw will be liquidated; and this city... that has blocked our path to the east for 700 years... will have ceased to exist."[3] With much of the city in Polish hands, however, Nazi commanders unleashed their forces on suburban areas where there had been little or no military activity. Chief among their units were two SS formations: SS-Sturmbrigade RONA, made up of Soviet deserters and commanded by a renegade Belarussian officer, and SS-Sturmbrigade Dirlewanger. The latter, commanded by Oskar Dirlewanger, a convicted child molester, was made up of convicts culled from German prisons: thieves, rapists, and murderers.

Unable to retake the central sections of the city, in the early days of August the Germans unleashed these units on civilians in the Ochota and Wola districts, killing almost every man, woman, and child. Women were raped, then slaughtered. Small children, including an entire pre-school captured by Dirlewanger's men, were often killed with bayonets and rifle butts.[4] Hospital patients were dragged from the beds and shot. Those too sick to move and infants in the maternity ward were doused with gasoline and burned alive. One survivor who was pregnant at the time lost her husband and all her children in the massacre at the Ursus tractor factory:

> They then began to set the houses on fire. I saw Nos. 35 and 8 in our street being set on fire; bottles of petrol were thrown into the flats without warning, and so it was impossible for the inhabitants to escape. I stayed in the cellar of No. 18 until August 5, when ... the Germans ordered all of us to get out, and marched us to Wolska Street. ... I went alone, accompanied only by my three children. It was difficult to pass, the road being full of wire, cable, remains of barricades, corpses, and rubble. Houses were burning on both sides of the street; I reached the Ursus works with great difficulty. Shots, cries, supplications and groans could be heard from the factory yard... The people who stood at the entrance were led, no,

pushed in, not all at once but in groups of 20. A boy of 12, seeing the bodies of his parents and of his little brother through the half-open entrance door, fell in a fit and began to shriek. The Germans and Vlassov's men beat him and pushed him back, while he was endeavoring to get inside. He called for his father and his mother. We all knew what awaited us here; there was no possibility of escape or of buying one's life; there was a crowd of Germans, Ukrainians (Vlassov's men), and cars. I came last and kept in the background, continuing to let the others pass, in the hope that they would not kill a pregnant woman, but I was driven in with the last lot. In the yard I saw heaps of corpses 3 ft high, in several places. The whole right and left side of the big yard (the first yard) was strewn with bodies. ... We were led through the second. There were about 20 people in our group, mostly children of 10–12. There were children without parents, and also a paralyzed old woman whose son-in-law had been carrying her all the time on his back. At her side was her daughter with two children of four and seven. They were all killed. The old woman was literally killed on her son-in-law's back, and he along with her. We were called out in groups of four and led to the end of the second yard to a pile of bodies. When the four reached this point, the Germans shot them through the backs of their heads with pistols. The victims fell on the heap, and others came. Seeing what was to be their fate, some attempted to escape; they cried, begged, and prayed for mercy. I was in the last group of four. I begged the Vlassov's men around me to save me and the children, and they asked if I had anything with which to buy my life. I had a large amount of gold with me and gave it them. They took it all and wanted to lead me away, but the German supervising the execution would not allow them to do so, and when I begged him to let me go he pushed me off, shouting "Quicker!" I fell when he pushed me. He also hit and pushed my elder boy, shouting "hurry up, you Polish bandit". Thus I came to the place of execution, in the last group of four, with my three children. I held my two younger children by one hand, and my elder boy by the other. The children were crying and praying. The elder boy, seeing the mass of bodies, cried out: "they are going to kill us" and called for his father. The first shot hit him, the second me; the next two killed the two younger children. I fell on my right side. The shot was not fatal. The bullet penetrated the back of my head from the right side and went out through my cheek. I spat out several teeth; I felt the left side of my body growing numb, but I was still conscious and saw everything that was going on around me.[5]

While the Germans found massacring civilians easy, retaking areas held by the Home Army proved far more difficult. Dirlewanger's men and their ex-Soviet counterparts were often incapable of carrying out attacks on Polish positions and suffered heavy losses. Mathias Schenk, an 18-year-old Belgian drafted as a Wehrmacht combat engineer, recalled:

We were constantly shot at. The next evening the infantry came to the rescue but we made no progress. Then an SS unit arrived. They looked strange. They had no ranks on their uniforms and reeked of vodka. They attacked instantly screaming hooorrraaay and were dying by the dozens. Their commander dressed in a black leather coat [Dirlewanger] was raging in the back pushing his men to attack. A tank arrived. We rushed with the SS troopers behind it. A few meters from the buildings the tank was hit. It exploded and a soldier's hat flew high up. We ran away again.[6]

German units frequently resorted to using civilians as human shields. Schenk remembered:

We were covering the front as the SS-men were rushing civilians out of their homes and positioning them around the tank, forcing some to sit on the armor. For the first time in my life I saw such a thing. They were speeding up a Polish woman in a long coat. She was holding a little girl in her arms. People crowded on the tank were helping her to climb up. Someone took the girl. When he was handing her back to the mother the tank started moving forward. The child fell down under the tracks and got crushed. The woman was screaming in terror. One of the SS-men frowned and shot the woman in the head. They continued driving. Those who tried to escape were killed by SS-men.[7]

With a vast superiority in heavy weapons, the Germans were able to drive the Poles back from many positions, but found them re-occupied as soon as the shelling stopped. Fighting their way through a maze of rubble-choked streets, even experienced Nazi units lost their way and suffered heavy losses. Julian Eugeniusz Kulski, a teenaged Home Army soldier in the Żoliborz district, hid in a building with his 40-man platoon. After shelling the building for a full day without seeing any reaction, the Germans decided it was empty and sent a large battle group of 375 SS men to attack a barricade behind Kulski's post.

The Germans approached our building and, after passing it, started the attack on the barricade. They soon realized that they had their hands full, and, since they were under continuous fire from the neighboring blocks of houses, they started to move slowly backwards. Only a few of them remained, firing at the barricade with their machine guns. Then came the long-awaited order to fire. We put the muzzles of our rifles, Sten guns, and machine guns forward through the windows, and poured a murderous fire down on the Germans, who were taken completely by surprise. In addition to this, the detachment on duty at the Health Center lost no time in firing on the enemy from the other side and launching an attack. One after another, the Germans were struck down by our bullets.

Positioned immediately under the window from which I was firing was an SS police machine-gun squad. At the first burst from Cadet-Officer 'Zawada's' Sten gun a machine-gunner was shot down. Although he was badly wounded, he tried to retreat, spitting blood and leaving a deadly red trail on the pavement. A rifle shot finished him off. He fell spread-eagled in the gutter. A few meters from him another policeman was lying with his stomach torn open by bullets. We did not spare ammunition when shooting at SS policemen—the men who had been responsible for the slaughter in the Ghetto, for the executions, the street hunts, and the wanton murders.[8]

Despite furious German attacks and serious losses, the Poles persisted, contesting the city block by block. At the same time, the Poles continued the fight to wipe out the remaining pockets of German holdouts inside the mostly Polish-held districts in the city. Home Army units launched repeated attacks on fortified German posts at the University of Warsaw, even using a homemade armored car, only to be beaten back with heavy losses. The Poles had better success in their attack on the state telephone exchange, known by its Polish acronym "PAST," one of Warsaw's few skyscrapers. The tall building, held by a detachment of SS men, served as an observation post for German artillery spotters and snipers. On August 20, after a siege of three weeks, the final assault on the PAST building began. Sapper units made up of teenaged girls spearheaded the attack, blowing holes in the thick concrete walls that shielded the SS defenders. Teams armed with homemade flamethrowers followed, driving the Nazis from their positions to be cut down by small-arms fire or surrender.

As the fighting raged around them, civilians took to living in basements and bomb shelters. The Home Army operated a system to distribute food and water and even had a postal service staffed by younger Boy Scouts and Girl Guides. Poles tried to maintain a semblance of normal life, and, freed from German repression, there were free cultural activities including poetry readings, concerts, theater, and even films.

Despite furious resistance, constant German pressure and the lack of supplies forced the defenders into a smaller area. Civilian losses mounted due to indiscriminate bombing and shelling. The Old Town sector, cut off from the City Center and the scene of some of the fiercest fighting, was under particularly intense pressure. At the end of August, Home

Army Command decided to evacuate the Old Town. Using the sewers, columns of soldiers, often wounded and exhausted, made a terrifying trip under the city. Risking German booby-traps and ambushes, young female couriers led the men to safety, often under the noses of the enemy. One of the couriers, Teresa Wilska, recalled:

> I am to lead the Wigry detachment; about 50 men... The sewer manhole is under heavy fire. Planes are bombing ceaselessly. Finally, the order is given. I lead and they jump in one after another. I have to wait quite a while, but finally they are all down. I tell them to take a count, but they swear and refuse.... After a long moment, they decide to do as bid. I instruct them that they must not use any lights nor do any talking in the sewer, for voices carry far ahead. They must follow each other in single file, I tell them, and there will be no swapping of places. We start. After a few minutes someone starts swearing. Flashlights are switched on. The din is getting louder by the minute. I stop and try to calm them down, but with a group of 50 guys who are in the sewers for the first time, that's no easy task.
>
> "What the hell, what are you?" I shout, raising my voice above the din. "A bunch of civilians, or what? Don't you understand when one talks to you? Silence! Right now or I'll blow off the head of the first one that talks."
>
> Wonder of wonders, it works. Did they become afraid? Or maybe they felt ashamed. All's quiet and we move ahead. In any event, my threat was quite ridiculously empty: I don't have a firearm, even one of the most puny kind.
>
> We reach the exit manhole. I climb out. Helping hands assist those who follow me.[9]

As this desperate battle raged through the streets of the Polish capital, the Allies looked on and debated what to do. The Soviets immediately denounced the Poles even though they had repeatedly called for just such an uprising. As the city fought, the Poles, the Germans, and the rest of the world knew that some outside help was needed to save the city.

CHAPTER 2

Aiding Warsaw

When the uprising began on August 1, the insurgents were successful in seizing control of almost two-thirds of left-bank Warsaw. Yet
the Germans mobilized local forces and poured in reinforcements in
response to Hitler's demand to exterminate Warsaw and its people. In
addition, the Polish insurgents faced increasingly painful problems with
weapons and supplies, eventually turning their fight into a hopeless
struggle for survival. The insurrectionists fought off the Germans at
isolated points of resistance. They suffered from shortages of not only
arms and ammunition, but also bandages, medicine, and food required
by the civilian population. Because of this, the Varsovians dramatically
implored the outside world for help. The first to face the challenge of
assisting Warsaw were the Polish and, later, British and South African
pilots operating from Allied airbases in Italy.

Up to that time, the missions of the special task divisions of the
Balkan Allied Air Force (BAAF),[1] which were to be employed in assisting Warsaw, had been limited to performing secret Special Operations
Executive (SOE)[2] missions over occupied Europe, which consisted of
dropping agents and supplies over designated sites. This practice stood
in clear opposition to the sudden necessity of organizing large-scale air
supply missions to a beleaguered city, which BAAF had never previously
carried out.

The missions to aid Warsaw quickly proved to be extremely dangerous
undertakings, demanding great experience and an almost reckless level

of courage, sacrifice, and bravado from the airmen. They were conducted under the cover of night and at quite low altitudes. There could be no room for the slightest errors or unanticipated limits of aircraft range. Often, the flights faced a dramatic climax in the smoke-draped sky above the burning city reminiscent of a giant camp fire. The heavy machines weighing many tons and loaded with supplies had to pass over the rooftops as rapidly as possible while avoiding the searchlights, the attacks of enemy night fighters, and the shells of anti-aircraft guns. Their crews attempted to locate the designated drop sites, where the insurrectionists were eagerly awaiting the badly needed supplies, while simultaneously struggling with a city landscape below that was difficult to identify and crisscrossed by a network of destroyed streets and squares.

The first information regarding the intended insurgent activities in Warsaw was passed on to the Main Transfer Base (*Główna Baza Przerzutowa*) in Italy via dispatches sent to its commander, Lt. Col. Marian Dorotycz-Malewicz "Hańcza," from the Commander-in-Chief of the Home Army, Gen. Tadeusz "Bór" Komorowski, which had been sent a few days following his initial decision to take the city, i.e., around July 27 and 29 (1944). In his radio messages, General "Bór" described the indispensable contents that would be needed in future airdrops and specified the rules of communication between the flight teams and the insurrectionists. At the same time, a similar message was also sent to the British War Office and the SOE Command.

The next dispatch from Warsaw to the Brindisi base arrived only after the fighting in the Polish capital had erupted. On August 2, Lieutenant Colonel Dorotycz-Malewicz was notified that the uprising in Warsaw had begun and, by extension, of the urgent necessity of delivering arms and ammunition to special locations in the city. Simultaneously, an initiative appealing for assistance for the uprising began. This consisted of mostly written pleas and lobbying undertaken on various levels of the exiled Polish governmental structure. The participants included: the president of Poland, Władysław Raczkiewicz; Poland's ambassador in London, Edward Raczyński; the Minister of National Defense, Gen. Marian Kukiel; the Chief-of-Staff of the Commander-in-Chief, Gen. Stanisław Kopański; the latter's deputy, Gen. Stanisław Tatar "Tabor";

and, following his return from Italy on August 6, 1944, the Commander-in-Chief, Gen. Kazimierz Sosnkowski, as well.

It quickly became apparent that Polish demands, such as the bombing of airfields near Warsaw, the dropping of the Polish Airborne Brigade,[3] or the transfer of fighter squadrons to the Warsaw area, would not materialize. This was confirmed before the start of the uprising by the British on July 28, 1944. In such a situation, the only remaining option may have been airdrops. However, when the fighting broke out, contrary to the logic of the events, neither the 148th Royal Air Force (RAF) Special Task Squadron, nor the Polish 1586th Special Task Squadron, was prepared to undertake such assignments. As far as the 1586th Squadron was concerned, some of the flight crews were leave-bound following earlier flights conducted mostly over Italy and Yugoslavia.[4] In terms of both aircraft quantity and technical quality, the condition of the unit's planes left much to be desired as well. On August 2, 1944 the squadron consisted of only about five flight crews and eight aircraft. During the first air operation over Warsaw, the mood prevalent among the squadron's flight crews was succinctly summarized by its commander, Major Eugeniusz Arciuszkiewicz, who stated that the attitudes were far from enthusiastic. The pilots were united by "a feeling of solidarity in performing their duty with a simultaneous and complete awareness of the hopelessness of the situation."[5]

On the third day of the rising, the commander of the 334th RAF Special Task Wing, Colonel W. E. Rankin, who was also the superior of the 1586th Squadron, and who had refused to earmark flight teams for Warsaw-bound flights, received permission to proceed from Gen. Colin Gubbins, the head of SOE, who had been lobbied by the Poles. This permission granted Rankin the autonomy to make the final decision independently. Thus, guided by the anticipated heavy losses and insignificant effects, he refused to free all the forces at his disposal for the missions. Simultaneously, Rankin allowed the Polish squadron, consisting of only three aircraft at the time, a completely free hand. The awareness of the purely symbolic nature of this gesture, fears of the total destruction of the 1586th Squadron, and deteriorating weather conditions meant that a mission utilizing the available resources was simply not carried out.

A similar fate befell Prime Minister Winston Churchill's permission—achieved as a result of President Raczkiewicz's pleadings—to conduct missions using RAF aircraft. It too was questioned by its recipient, the commander of the RAF in the Mediterranean, Marshal John Slessor. Utilizing his prerogative to make the binding decision regarding the use of air squadrons under his command, Slessor refused. He also pointed out that the Soviets were much closer to Warsaw and, therefore, in a much better position to assist.

Slessor eventually became a symbol of opposition toward implementing a plan to aid the Warsaw Uprising.[6] To understand the causes of his position, it may be worthwhile to examine his memoirs, contained in his autobiographic *The Central Blue*, which dealt with the entire duration of the war. Slessor also dedicated a few pages to the Polish uprising of August 1944. When mentioning this event, he, on the one hand, affirms his friendly attitude toward the Poles and admires their courage and bravery, which he witnessed throughout the conflict. On the other hand, his attitude towards the Poles' political decisions makes clear that he viewed them as tragically imprudent, tactless, and even outright stupid. The period of the Warsaw Uprising was, as Slessor admits, one of his worst life experiences. Having approached the issue in a purely rationalist manner over a period of several weeks, Slessor weighed the risks and benefits of using his forces to aid Warsaw, and the balance always appeared negative. At the same time, it was difficult for him to abandon this line of reasoning and reconcile himself with the fact that he could succumb to political pressure that was, in his opinion, irrational.

Eventually, Slessor emerged from this trying time with great admiration for the efforts and sacrifices of the flight crews, along with a very negative and emotive opinion of the Soviets: "I hope that a special hell exists for the bastards from the Kremlin, who betrayed Bor's army and caused an unnecessary sacrifice of about 200 airmen of the 205th Group and the 334th Wing."[7]

Because precious time was elapsing and the inclement weather improved on August 4, the chief of the Transfer Base, Major Jan Jaźwiński, and the commander of the 1586th Squadron, Major Arciuszkiewicz, utilized the fact that flights to Poland had not been forbidden entirely and, in agreement with the flight crews, chose to take advantage of it. Under the pretext of preparing flights to other locations in Poland, while maintaining the utmost secrecy before the British, four flight crews were earmarked which were to reach Warsaw in spite of all obstacles. Three of the crews conducted the first drop above the city on the night of August 4–5. Airmen from the RAF's 148th Special Task Squadron who took off for Poland on that very same night were not as lucky as the Poles. Because they incurred losses, and four crews failed to return to base, Marshal Slessor suspended British flights to Poland until August 12.

Concurrently, also on August 4, Prime Minister Churchill sent a message to Stalin, informing the Soviet dictator of the fighting in Warsaw and British plans to assist. Stalin replied the next day, dismissing both the importance of the events in Warsaw, as well as the chances of the insurgents who, in his opinion, were organized in fictional military structures which failed to correspond to reality. Not one sentence addressed any possible role for the Red Army in aiding the insurrection.

The following day the BAAF Command issued an order forbidding completely all flights to Poland. The stated reason was the expected losses. At the same time, the order suggested that flights take place at moonless times, i.e., only 10 times per month. In the context of the fighting in Warsaw, such a decision was unacceptable to the Poles. The Polish base once again considered assigning fictitious drop points. On August 6, however, the British government, under Polish pressure, decided not to hold Marshal Slessor responsible for the Varsovian missions.[8] Because Slessor refused to send out British units until the moon was in its last quarter, the Air Force Minister in charge of the RAF, Archibald Sinclair, waived the ban on flights to Poland, but emphasized that only Poles could embark on them.

With permission secured, all three flight crews at the disposal of the 1586th Squadron were dispatched to Warsaw on the night of August 8–9. The Germans did not yet have sufficient time to prepare and consolidate their defenses around the city. Hence, all the flight crews managed to drop their cargos successfully. According to Slessor, this fed deluded Polish hopes and intensified their lobbying efforts on behalf of Warsaw. The following night, the squadron's four flight crews once again headed for Poland, their cargos intended not for Warsaw, but for fighters stationed in the nearby Kampinos Forest (*Puszcza Kampinoska*).

From the moment the fighting began, the staff of the Commander-in-Chief received daily dispatches from General "Bór" demanding "aid in ammunition and anti-tank weaponry immediately and within the following days [as well]."[9] These were written in an alarming, bitter, and openly recriminatory tone. Apart from an emotional and heart-wrenching call for help, the dispatches also reflect a surprisingly small degree of familiarity with last-minute information about the British attitude toward the uprising and a poor ability to assess the situation, in spite of a plethora of analytical materials compiled over the previous years of the war.

The same tone is apparent in other dispatches sent from Warsaw at the time, which were either sent directly to the base, or those sent by the staff of the Commander-in-Chief. An often-cited radio message sent on August 10 to the commander of the 1586th Squadron may serve as an example of the latter. In it, the usually cool and sober General Sosnkowski speaks of the necessity of immediate airdrops for Warsaw, regardless of circumstances, the danger of losing aircraft, or the perils awaiting their airmen, who would be forced to parachute from the downed machines to survive.

In addition to earlier efforts, attempts to secure aid for the rising were also undertaken by the Polish Prime-Minister-in-Exile, Stanisław Mikołajczyk. He had been searching for a way to compromise with the Soviet Union, and happened to be on an official visit in Moscow on July 31, 1944. He lobbied for assistance as soon as possible and informed London about the results of his talks in Moscow on August 10. This message stated that, during a meeting taking place the previous day, Stalin had provided only vague assurance that he would aid the rising through airdrops. Trusting Stalin's words, Mikołajczyk requested that London Poles inform the Soviets of the current positions held by the insurgents. He also declared that a Soviet staff officer would soon be inserted into rebel-held Warsaw to coordinate this apparently promising Polish–Soviet cooperation.

Meanwhile, the 1586th Squadron did not receive British permission to carry out new missions over Warsaw. Its commander once again contemplated the trick of employing fictitious drop points in Poland to secretly supply the capital. This idea was quickly made irrelevant by the deterioration of the weather, which canceled all flights.

In a subsequent message sent on August 12 to Stalin, Churchill informed him succinctly of the continued fighting in Warsaw. He was basing his message on information originating from the Plenipotentiary of the [Polish] Government (*Delegat Rządu*), Jan Jankowski, and dispatched from Warsaw to the Polish authorities in London. Quite sure of the weight of his message, as well as the difficulties he was experiencing, he asked in conclusion: "They are asking for machine guns and ammunition. Can you help them, given that the distance from Italy is so great?"[10]

As the testimonies of many contemporaries show, Churchill, often ruthless and, in his own way, pragmatically indifferent toward the Polish Question, became emotionally invested in the Warsaw Uprising throughout its duration. On the one hand, information regarding the heroism of the Poles awakened his admiration. On the other, news of German barbarity intensified his anger toward the Nazis and irritation toward the callous Stalin.

On the following day, Prime Minister Mikołajczyk once again turned to Stalin. Following up on the recent meeting of August 9 and the declaration then offered by Stalin, he once again requested air assistance for Warsaw. He hoped that the Soviets would bomb airfields and armored trains operating in the city, and also asked the Soviets to provide daytime cover and airdrops of arms and ammunition. In his dispatch, the Polish prime minister also pointed out that it was in the Soviets' interest to take the city as liberators, rather than simply "clearing the rubble and burying the dead," which would impact future Polish–Soviet relations accordingly.[11]

After a temporary hiatus, and having once again secured permission, a total of 11 aircraft took off for Warsaw on the night of August 12–13. This included five Polish bombers and six British ones of the 148th RAF Squadron, which was once again directed into action, but had not previously flown missions over Warsaw. The airdrops were conducted by four Polish air crews and three British ones. In spite of intense enemy anti-aircraft defense, the Allies incurred no losses this time.

Simultaneously, as a result of the decision made under the influence of Winston Churchill himself, another large-scale mission was being planned. The nights between August 12 and 17 were moonless, which, according to Slessor, and in accordance with the heretofore employed practice of air mission planning, increased flight safety. For the purposes of the mission, Marshal Slessor withdrew two air squadrons from the 205th Bomber Group (178th RAF Squadron and 31st South African Air Force [SAAF] Squadron) from the planned amphibious Operation *Dragoon* and redirected them to carry aid to Warsaw.[12] On the night of August 13–14, a taskforce consisting of 20 aircraft of the 205th Bomber Group, four Polish machines from the 1586th Squadron, and four additional ones from the 148th RAF Squadron, headed for Warsaw. Three Polish air crews, seven British, and four South African ones participated in the drop. This time, the Germans managed to shoot down one British air crew from the 178th RAF Squadron and two from the 31st SAAF Squadron.

As Stalin's cynical game appeared increasingly clear to him, Churchill cabled his Foreign Secretary, Anthony R. Eden, on August 14, ordering an intensification of the latter's activities:

> It is quite puzzling that, at a moment when the underground army launched an uprising, the Russian armies halted their offensive on Warsaw and withdrew a certain distance. For them, the sending of ammunition and machine guns, which the Poles require for their heroic struggle, means only a 100-mile flight. I spoke to Air Marshal Slessor, attempting to organize supply deliveries from here, in the greatest quantities possible. But what are the Russians doing?
>
> I believe that it will be good if you sent a message to Stalin through Molotov, pointing out all the implications of their passivity, and demanding that they help as much as possible.[13]

A subsequent mission, this time consisting of 26 aircraft, departed the following night. Because of the strong anti-aircraft defenses, all of the air crews could not perform the airdrops over the designated locations. Six British and four South African crews succeeded over Warsaw, but the remaining two Polish teams were forced to drop their cargos over the Kampinos Forest. As a result of the mission, three planes of the 178th RAF Squadron were lost, in addition to one of the 148th RAF

Squadron, three of the 31st SAAF Squadron, and one Polish air crew. Yet, time has shown that the mission on the night of August 14–15 was the most effective in terms of the number of drops actually received by the insurgents. Unfortunately, the losses convinced Marshal Slessor to once again suspend direct Warsaw-bound flights. Thus, aircraft departing on the night of August 15–16 delivered supplies only outside of the city limits. The British, South African, and Polish airmen completed their missions successfully, albeit with differing results.

Simultaneously, Slessor responded to the constant Polish pleas for airstrikes by his forces on targets in Warsaw. He stated that such an option was unfeasible, but, at the same time, advised turning to the 8th United States Army Air Force (USAAF), which was stationed in Britain and conducted daytime air operations. Slessor argued in the same vein during his meeting with Churchill, which took place during the second half of August, during the latter's visit to Italy. The air marshal strove to persuade the prime minister that involving the Americans not only in bombing strikes, but also in airdrops for the insurrectionists, constituted the only sensible option given the circumstances.

During the night of August 16–17 a total of 18 aircraft took off for Poland. Their destination was not Warsaw, however, but the adjacent Kampinos Forest. The airdrop was conducted by three Polish air crews and elements of British and South African crews. Three crews from the 31st SAAF Squadron and two from the Polish squadron were downed. The following night, a successful airdrop over the Kabacki Forest was carried out by only one Polish crew. The remaining three crews which took off at the time were unable to carry out their mission for various reasons.

During the time period under discussion, the 1586th Squadron experienced an influx of new and inexperienced air crews, which were to replace the crews lost during the previous missions. Time constraints did not permit sufficient training of these replacements, and their effectiveness proved minimal and inversely proportional to the risk of their loss. The equipment, whose very limits had been tested through constant use, presented an additional, constant, and increasing source of trouble. Attempts were made to tentatively remedy this problem through hasty repairs and by borrowing machines from other squadrons. Thus, Halifax bombers from other units, often in atrocious technical condition, were employed.

On August 17, the BAAF Command halted airdrops into Warsaw, only to withdraw the 148th RAF Squadron completely from Poland-bound flights. Only Polish volunteer airmen could now risk their lives in performing these dangerous missions. In accord with this decision, only the 1586th Squadron carried out the missions. During the next two nights (August 20–21 and 21–22), its crews conducted one airdrop into Warsaw and two in the Kampinos Forest per night. Following an unsuccessful attempt to reach Warsaw on the night of August 22–23, the three subsequent nights saw airdrops onto targets located only within the Kampinos Forest. Yet another attempt, on the night of August 26–27, was not only a failure, but also resulted in the loss of two Polish air crews.

In spite of the great efforts and risks involved, the airdrops over the Kampinos Forest may be viewed as only a partial success. From the beginning of the rising, the Polish units operating in the city and the Kampinos Forest were separated by German forces and could not communicate with each other freely. Thus, drops into the forest, although welcomed with great joy, failed to change the situation of the insurgents within the capital itself.

Only on the night of August 27–28 did the unit manage to conduct a successful airdrop into Warsaw. Unfortunately, like in previous cases, the price paid for this success was the loss of two more Polish air crews. As a result, the commander of the BAAF, Vice Marshal William Elliot, banned the Poles from conducting more missions, while Slessor canceled all flights.

Yet the matter remained open. On August 31, Marshal Portal turned to Slessor regarding the possibility of resuming the missions while utilizing delaying mechanisms used for parachutes. The goal was to conduct the drops from a higher altitude to avoid enemy anti-aircraft fire.

The flights were once again resumed on the night of September 1–2. Supplies were dropped into both the Radom-Kielce district (to the south of Warsaw) and the Kampinos Forest. The action resulted in the loss of four Polish air crews. The effect was another suspension of flights, this time lasting until September 10. A report written at roughly the same time, by Air Force General Ludomił Rayski, the Delegate of the Commander of the (Polish) Air Force with the Mediterranean Allied Air Force (MAAF), shows the gravity of the situation. The document describes the situation in Warsaw, as well as the effects of the Allied aid efforts. Rayski, who had himself participated in two airdrop missions and was intimately familiar with their nature, states that "the English are striving to accommodate us as much as possible" but are unable to further tolerate such high losses which fail to translate into acceptable results. He also mentions that:

> In the case of operations over Germany, the losses range from 3–5%. In the operations over Poland they reach 30%. The country (*Kraj*, i.e. Poland) notifies us that many planes do not reach the destination, and many airdrops fall into German hands. … This is a suicidal massacre (*wybijanie*) of airmen.[14]

On the night of September 10, following an extensive hiatus, the first significant air expedition, with the additional participation of British and South African air crews, headed for Poland. It was also the first flight utilizing the previously mentioned parachute delaying mechanisms. The mission consisted of five Polish crews, eight British ones from the 178th and 148th RAF Squadrons, and 10 South African crews from the 31th and 34th SAAF Squadrons. During the flight, significant cloud cover proved a major obstacle, impeding the proper identification of the drop zones. Four British and two South African air crews dropped their cargos over Warsaw, although the effects were difficult to predict. One Polish and one South African crew delivered their cargos over the Kampinos Forest. The 34th SAAF Squadron and the 148th RAF Squadron lost one air crew each while the Poles lost three.

Once again, British airmen were banned from participating in Poland-bound missions as a result of the losses, although the Poles still retained the right. On the night of September 13–14, during the last Warsaw-bound flight for the duration of the uprising, only one air crew reached the city. A second one, dispatched the same night, failed to drop its cargo and was shot down over Hungary while returning to its home base.

The two final flights to Poland conducted during the insurrection occurred in the second half of September. During the first one, on the night of September 18–19, five air crews of the 34th SAAF Squadron took off for Warsaw. They were recalled from their mission before reaching the coast of Yugoslavia, however. From among the six aircraft taking off that night, only two crews dropped their cargos in areas outside of Warsaw.

Another air expedition took place on the night of September 21–22. Twelve machines with Polish, British, and South African airmen participated. However, the airdrop was conducted only over areas forming the operating base of the Home Army "Kampinos Group." This underground unit was crushed by the Germans a week later near the locality of Jaktorów near Warsaw.

During the period of August 4–5 to September 13–14, 1944, the Polish 1586th Squadron conducted 14 airdrops over Warsaw, 29 over the Kampinos Forest, and one over the Kabacki Forest. A total of 73 airmen perished, 18 were captured by the enemy, and 12 were rescued by the partisans, allowing some to make their way back to their units. The missions resulted in a total of 15 downed aircraft. In this context, it is important to keep in mind that, as of August 2, 1944, the 1586th Squadron included five air crews and eight airplanes. Thus, the losses constituted about 200% of the unit's original state, which meant that the squadron twice ceased to exist.

At the time, Warsaw-bound missions were flown by other units as well. Their losses were as follows:

- 148th RAF Squadron: two aircraft lost, 10 airmen killed, three airmen captured;
- 178th RAF Squadron: four aircraft lost, 27 airmen killed, one airman captured;
- 31st SAAF Squadron: eight aircraft lost, 40 airmen killed, seven airmen captured, one airman rescued by Home Army, 12 airmen rescued by Soviets;
- 34th SAAF Squadron: one aircraft lost, five airmen killed, two airmen captured.

In total, as a result of the airdrop operation for Warsaw and its vicinity, the PAF, RAF, and SAAF jointly lost 30 aircraft, 155 killed airmen, and

31 captured airmen, while 25 were rescued by the Polish partisans or Soviet soldiers.

Based on analyses produced by the Special Department (*Oddział Specjalny*) of the staff of the Commander-in-Chief, it is estimated (keeping in mind the margin of error) that the total number of airdrops conducted by the PAF, RAF, and SAAF amounts to:

- For Warsaw: 30 airdrops between August 4 and September 13;
- For the Kampinos and Kabacki Forests: 28 airdrops between August 4 and September 21.[15]

This counts the number of drops, not the number of containers delivered. Thus, altogether, 58 airdrops were carried out, which constitutes approximately 70% of all the drops which the Allied air forces managed to conduct over the targeted areas.

CHAPTER 3

Mission to Warsaw

In the early morning hours of Monday, September 18, American airbases in Suffolk and Cambridgeshire hummed with intense aircraft maintenance work. Mechanics conducted last-minute inspections of the airplanes, which were refueled and loaded anew with weaponry and ammunition. Meanwhile, the air crews were roused from their beds at 0300 to eat breakfast and gather their equipment, consisting of oxygen masks, parachutes, and emergency landing kits. Afterwards they were led to briefings conducted separately by some air crew members, including the pilots, bombardiers, navigators, and radio operators.

The pilots of the 355th Fighter Group were initially briefed on September 12. Some of the items discussed were the general political and military situation in Warsaw and the tasks the unit would be expected to perform. The airmen were ordered to leave behind their side arms and not to discuss political subjects with the Soviets. If emergency landing over Soviet-controlled territory was necessary, the pilots were told to remain in their cockpits and not undertake any independent actions. The air crews were also warned of the presence of Soviet fighters, which were to operate below the level of the bombers.

To provide any necessary assistance and coordination, the 100th Bomber Group was joined by intelligence officer Danny M. Lewis of the 355th Fighter Group, and technical officer, Captain E. H. McMillan of the 358th Fighter Squadron.

The course of events that transpired during the early morning hours of September 18 at one of the American bomber bases was reported by the pilot, Captain M. W. Kowalski, in *Dziennik Polski i Dziennik Żołnierza* [The Polish Daily and Soldier's Daily]. The author recalled that the captain giving the briefing stated the goal and route of the mission and elaborated:

> Today's expedition is the direct result of our President's conference with Prime Minister Churchill in Quebec. They both arrived at the common conclusion that it is necessary to resume aiding Warsaw. Our bomber division has participated in these kinds of missions three times already, having conducted weapon and ammunition drops for the French Maquis. You surely remember how generously you were rewarded with the results gained for the assistance you provided to the French Underground Army. Today your help is once again needed, this time by Warsaw, which has been fighting the Germans for many weeks and is now desperately short of arms and ammunition. Above Warsaw you will meet up with Soviet fighters, and you will land in Russia after carrying out the mission.[1]

Next, the speaker informed the pilots that supplies will be dropped onto two locations, and that the aircraft were divided into two groups, each of which was assigned to one of the two zones. At the time, the airmen were presented with a map of Warsaw indicating which parts of the city were controlled by the Home Army and how to successfully identify these. Afterwards, the same officer described the expected meteorological conditions in Warsaw. According to forecasts, the only problems were to be expected in Britain, where the dense fog covering the airfields might hamper the taxiing and take-off. The predicted time of arrival above the drop zones in Warsaw was between 1300 and 1400 h, after which the planes were to land in Soviet-held territory around 1600 h.[2]

The briefing also included standard information about the engine starting time, the taxiing order, the radio frequencies to be employed, the approach path, the starting points, and the flight path itself.

Following the meeting the air crews were introduced to the commander of the Polish Air Force, Brigadier General Mateusz Iżycki, who addressed the pilots:

> In the name of the Polish Government and the Polish Air Force I arrived to visit you on the day in which America is bringing aid to Warsaw. This day, which has

been awaited by millions in Poland, is undoubtedly a historic one. Warsaw has been fighting for 48 days, and has reached the limits of its endurance. The aid which you are bringing may well prove decisive in saving many human lives and may yet contribute to the eventual victory. I am certain that you will perform your job well. I wish you "good luck" [in original English] in your mission![3]

The general's words were greeted with applause. As the reporter states: "The crews prepared to carry out this mission with great zeal and enthusiasm. The adventure attracted them with the enormity of the task and its uncommon nature." At the end of the meeting Col. Karl Truesdell Jr., commander of the expedition, spoke:

> I am not a historian … But we all know the name of Kościuszko, who was a Pole and took part in the war to liberate America. Today you have the opportunity to show your gratitude to Poland for what he did for America back then. I am sure that we will all gladly take advantage of this opportunity.

After the conclusion of the briefing the crews were driven to their aircraft. Dressed in many layers and encumbered by parachutes, the airmen took their seats in the planes, but not without some effort. Soon, the routine procedure of starting the engines and checking the radios began. Finally, the machines slowly approached the runways and taxied, taking off at 30-s increments.

Between 0600 and 0620 h, 110 Boeing B-17 "Flying Fortress" bombers belonging to the 3rd Bomber Division of the 13th Bomber Wing of the 8th USAAF took off from the eighth Air Force's British airfields. The expedition consisted of three bomber groups, the 95th, 100th, and 390th, escorted by elements of three fighter groups, the fourth, 355th, and 361st.

The Boeing B-17 "Flying Fortress" was the basic American heavy bomber. Its G version, introduced in September 1943, was the model produced in the greatest numbers during the war. Built in accordance with the American conception of daytime bombing in large formations, the powerful four-engine machine was made entirely of metal and boasted a 32-m wing span and measured 23 m in length. It was armed with twelve .50 caliber machine guns installed in eight gun emplacements. The plane's range was about 3,000 km and its maximum speed about 486 km/h. The large bomb chamber, capable of fitting approximately 2,700 kg of bombs, contained about 6–12 standard British containers. Based on photographs taken during the mission, these were type-C metal containers with lengthwise openings and characteristic shock-absorber endings, in addition to their type-H equivalents, which consisted of five parts, and were designed to fit smaller items. Their number depended on whether the aircraft was the head airplane leading each bomber division in a bomber group, a so-called Pathfinder, an ordinary bomber, or an aircraft carrying baggage in its bomb chamber in addition to containers.[4] The containers measured almost 180 cm in length, 40 cm in diameter, and weighed about 100 kg each. The supplies they carried were as follows.

Supplies Earmarked for Warsaw, Operation Frantic 7 *(by source)*

Item/type	Garliński/Zawodny[5]	USSAFE records[6]
Sten machine guns	2,976	2,987
Bren machine guns	211	390
Revolvers	545	545
Sten gun ammunition	1,691,400	
Bren gun ammunition	548,600	882,050 rounds
Pistol ammunition	27,250	
Mk. I Piat anti-tank grenade-launchers	110	102
Piat rounds	2,200	2,040
Gammon grenades	2,490	
Other grenades	4,360	7,070
Anti-tank mines	n/a	10
Plastic explosives	7,865 kg	16,070 lbs
Explosive fuses	54,400 meters	
Gunpowder fuses	8,720 m	7,120 lbs
Detonators	21,990 pieces	
Canned meat	23,520 cans	
Canned dry biscuits	2,016 cans	30,290 pieces
Margarine	915 kg	($\frac{2}{3}$ standard food;
American K rations[7]	5,820	$\frac{1}{3}$ special food)
Powdered milk	5,820 packages	
Medical equipment	12 containers	2,420 pieces

Supplies Earmarked for Warsaw by Number of Containers

Type	Containers[*]
Plastic and other explosive materials	89
Grenades, Sten guns, ammunition, and small arms	109
Small arms ammunition	101
Bren machine guns with ammunition	417
Piat anti-tank grenade-launchers and grenades	102
Standard food	184
Special food (as requested by the Poles)	64
Grenades (as requested by the Poles)	3
Medical supplies (as requested by the Poles)	11

[*] Some of the containers were prepared by the Poles. Their number is unknown.[8]

In addition to containers, the bomb chambers of all the "Flying Fortresses" were also fitted with four 75-gallon fuel tanks, which were used in fighter planes, and were necessary for such a long flight.

After take-off, the bombers initially headed toward an indicated radio beacon. Afterwards, they climbed to a required altitude and proceeded to an assigned spot in the formation after locating their groups. The rendezvous of the divisions belonging to various bomber groups occurred at an altitude of 4,000 ft above the home bases. Division A, which had been circling above the airbase, was joined by Divisions B and C. Once completely formed, the groups followed their Pathfinders and joined the expedition's battle formation, which had been forming above the coastal town of Southwold.[9] From this point, around 0730 h, the aircraft began climbing, in 2-min increments, to an altitude of 14,000 ft and headed for Warsaw.

Until the expedition reached the enemy coastline, it was kept abreast of the weather forecast by two P-51 fighters, which received the radio codename of "Kodak White," and flew 10 min in advance of the air armada.

The planned duration of the expedition, from its take-off at zero hour (0730) until reaching the Soviet bases, was about 8 h and 25 min.[10] This meant that the airmen would spend about 11 h (including 4–5 h using oxygen masks) in their machines if we calculate the time devoted to take-off, formation, and landing in the Soviet airfields. After completing their missions, the formations making up the expedition would land in Eastern Command bases in Soviet-occupied Ukraine to the southeast of Kyiv in Poltava (95th Bomber Group and part of the 390th Bomber Group), Mirgorod (100th Bomber Group and the remainder of the 390th), and Piriatyn (355th Fighter Group). These airfields were located 1,800 miles (2,897 km) from Britain.

The expedition was preceded by a De Havilland Mosquito reconnaissance plane belonging to the 653rd Light Bomber Squadron.[11] Before the first group of bombers appeared over the city, the Mosquito reached Warsaw 20 min. in advance, conveying information on the weather, cloud top height, and the activity of enemy fighters near the flight path.

The crew of the machine codenamed "Maypole Three" consisted of pilot, Lt. Robert Peterson, and navigator, R. C. E. Smith. As Smith noted in his logbook, they encountered a storm front in the Warsaw area. This information was immediately radioed to the air fleet. On reaching the city at an altitude of 25,000 ft, the two noticed three enemy aircraft flying below, at a height of 17,000 ft, which began climbing toward them. To avoid an unwelcome encounter Lieutenant Peterson increased the speed of his Mosquito. With the benefit of superior speed the plane continued to follow its designated flight path and reached Poltava.

Based on a previous understanding, on September 17 the Head Command of the Home Army received a radio message, which was later confirmed by the melody of "Jeszcze jeden mazur dzisiaj" ("One more Mazur today") played after the Polish-language BBC program at 2300 h.[12] Thus, the units tasked with intercepting the drops in Warsaw were placed on high alert. Around 1000 h the following day, the head of the 6th Department of the staff of the Commander-in-Chief informed the commander of the Home Army of the departure of the expedition through a dispatch later confirmed by the melody "Hej Madziar Pije" ("Hey, the Magyar Drinks") which followed the morning BBC programming. The message stated: "At dawn over one-hundred fortresses, along with an escort, once again took off in your direction. Expect [them] around 12 [o'clock] MEZ.[13] They won't bomb. The containers will be in the air for 7 min, hence a great dispersal."[14]

Units in districts still held by the insurrectionists were now being informed of the airdrop. Lacking other options, information regarding drops over the Mokotów and Żoliborz districts of Warsaw was conveyed to the proper units by radio via London.

At 0759 h two reserve bombers (42-31987, pilot: John K. Furrer/42-97673, pilot: Lloyd G. Delaney) belonging to the 100th Bomber Group turned around above the North Sea. Soon thereafter, at 0916 h, another aircraft from the same group was forced to return before reaching the Danish coast due to engine problems (42-31066, pilot: Warren G. McCoy).

The initial part of the journey proceeded according to plan without encountering any problems. During this time the planes constituting the formation flew over the North Sea, Schleswig Holstein (Control Point 1st Schleswig), and the Danish island of Lolland (Control Point 2nd Maribo).[15] As Division B of the 390th Bomber Group passed over the Danish Peninsula, its crews observed chaotic anti-aircraft fire to the north of the flight path originating from the area of Flensburg. The fire was believed to be coming from a ship. The armada continued its flight over the Baltic Sea, Koszalin (reached during Control Point 3), Chojnice, and Chełmno.

Along the way the bombers were accompanied by 154 P-51 Mustang fighters, dubbed "Little Friends" by bomber crews, which belonged to the 361st (8th Air Force, 1st Bomber Division, 67th Fighter Wing) and the 4th and 355th Fighter Group (8th Air Army, 2nd Bomber Division, 65th Fighter Wing). The planes had already earned their reputation as the war's best fighters. Superior armament, maneuverability, speed reaching 700 km/h, and a range of over 3,000 km, were highly prized by the pilots and made the machines a powerful instrument in the battle against the enemy.

The escort accompanying the expedition, commanded by Capt. John D. Duncan in the first phase of the mission, consisted of 43 Mustangs of the 361st Fighter Group "The Yellow Jackets." The fighters took off from Britain at 0740 h. Their rendezvous with the bombers occurred 2 h later, at an altitude of 15,000 ft, near the town of Kappeln on the eastern coast of the Danish Peninsula. Planes of the 361st Fighter Group accompanied the bombers until 1044 h, concluding their mission in the area of Bornholm Island, about 35 miles to the north of Kołobrzeg (Kolberg).

During the course of the mission, the pilots of the 361st Fighter Group saw, as the extant report indicates, the aircraft belonging to the 4th Fighter Group, but did not encounter the machines of the 355th Fighter Group. On the way back, at an altitude of 10,000 ft, a lone German Heinkel He-111 was spotted and subsequently destroyed in a rapid attack. At 1105 h, in turn, 20 moored hydroplanes were noticed on the coast. An assault dispatched a multi-engine hydroplane which, based on the report, was most likely a six-engine Blohm und Voss Bv 222 Viking. Twenty minutes later, half a mile north of Jagel, a mock airfield, prepared by the Germans to deceive the enemy, was spotted.

Within the next few minutes, at 1130 h, a group of six departing Messerschmitt Me-109s were sighted near Schleswig at a height of 10,000 ft. Two were shot down as a result of an immediate decision to attack.

At 1127 h a taxiing Me 109 fighter was observed by pilots of the 361st Group at Jagel airfield, 5 miles south of Schleswig. The enemy plane was quickly destroyed. Of 15 other such aircraft at the airfield, two were destroyed and six more damaged. The Flak fire encountered during this action was light and moderately accurate.[16] This was the last time during which the aircraft piloted by 2nd Lt. Clyde A. Arrants (Mustang P-51 D-5-NA, serial no. 44-13949) was seen by his fellow airmen from the 374th Fighter Squadron. As the report suggests, it was most likely shot down by the Germans during this action.

A dozen or so minutes later, three German Me 109 fighters were seen above Löwenstedt. They were pursued but eventually managed to wriggle away. In this region the crew encountered intensive Flak fire and noted six red flares shot in the area of Eckernförde Bay. The aircraft of the 361st Fighter Group concluded their mission by landing at 1319 h.[17]

A group of 39 planes from the 4th Fighter Group "The Eagles" met the bombers between 0910 and 0920 h between Heligoland and Westerhever at an altitude of 15–18,000 ft.[18] The duration of its escort duty passed without any incidents and ended between Rummelsburg and Chojnice around 1118 h.[19] In the reports completed at the end of *Frantic 7* the support provided by these two fighter groups was assessed as excellent.

The rendezvous of the bombers with an escort consisting of 64 aircraft belonging to the 355th Fighter Group "The Steeple Morden Strafers," which had been flying over northern Germany until that point, occurred with a 20-min delay at 1145 h at an altitude of 17–19,000 ft to the north of Toruń (Control Point 4).[20]

The 355th Group was initially headed by Col. Everett W. Stewart from the 354th Fighter Squadron, but, soon after crossing the English Channel, a generator failure forced him to return to base. His duties were assumed by the simultaneous commander of the Borax Squadron, Maj. Bert W. Marshall.[21] Soon thereafter, the 354th Squadron was led by Maj. Charles W. Lenfest, "Chuck." The remaining two squadrons were commanded by Maj. John L. Elder (357th Fighter Squadron) and Maj. Emil L. Sluga (358th Fighter Squadron).[22] The escorting aircraft flew 2,000 ft above the bombers, which remained unchallenged until coming into contact with the enemy to the north of Warsaw.

Halfway along the path to Szczecin (Stettin), near Lake Steinhuder located to the north of Hannover, the bomber commander informed the 355th Group of an expected 15-min delay. Thus, to avoid attracting unnecessary enemy attention and to save fuel, Major Marshall decided that the fighters would slow down, rather than circle around the Rendezvous Point (RP) near Koszalin. After 20 min, he received a surprising radio communiqué that the bombers would arrive at the RP 15 min early.

The situation forced Major Marshall to decide quickly to designate another RP, which would entail a rendezvous with the bombers on the other side of an atmospheric front stretching between Szczecin and Toruń. The eventual rendezvous took place at 1145 h above Bydgoszcz at a height of 14,000 ft. In spite of these difficulties, a sufficient amount of fuel allowed the fighters to continue their escorting duties. Unfortunately, the misunderstanding regarding the rendezvous time also brought the fighters closer to the well-defended port city of Szczecin. As a result, they encountered a heavy and accurate anti-aircraft barrage. Hence, several of the 358th's Mustangs were damaged. Due to a damaged cockpit windshield of a Mustang belonging to the 357th Squadron (Mustang P-51 D, serial no. 44-64068), Capt. Harold J. Hoffman suffered a right-arm wound, but managed to nevertheless continue piloting his machine.

Having reached the area of Toruń, the expedition encountered an atmospheric front which, as it later turned out, delayed the completion of the mission by 30 min. At this point, in order to climb above the cloud cover, each group began to ascend by performing 360° turns. Unfortunately, having reached an altitude of 20,800 ft, the fighters informed the bombers that the cloud level ended only at the altitude of 30,000 ft. The formations now descended below the cloud level and continued at this lower altitude.

The 390th Bomber Group encountered the clouds of the weather front around 1141 h. At this point, the group performed three 360° turns: two attempts to rise above the cloud cover (to the altitude of 20,000 ft) and, upon their failure, one descent (by Division A) to the level of 14,000 ft to continue below the cloud level. The three divisions forming the 390th Group[23] would continue the rest of the mission at the following altitudes: 14,000 ft (A), 15,000 (B), and 13,000 (C).

While performing the climbing maneuver, at 1159 h, at the altitude of 17,000 ft, Lieutenant Edwards' (42-102951) team, part of Division A of the 95th Bomber Group leading the expedition, was forced to drop its containers as a result of the failure of engine four. Thus lightened, the machine could continue on its path without abandoning its place in the formation. However, the dropped containers forced the 390th Group, which was the last unit in the formation, to perform a sharp turn to avoid collision. The crews watched the parachutes fall in the area of 53 02 N, 19 07 E (Toruń, Brodnica, Rypin). As was later suspected, this incident revealed the destination and objective of the expedition to the enemy and was the most likely culprit attracting the German fighters that intercepted the armada.

At probably the same time the local Oberkommando der Luftwaffe (OKL) post in Kętrzyn (Rastenburg, Masuria/East Prussia) sent a report warning and alerting its subordinate units: "250 four-engine bombers are heading in the direction of Pomerania. Expected arrival time in the area of Warsaw at 1315 h."[24]

Most likely because of this information the expedition was also mentioned in a transcript of telephone conversations conducted by the staff of the 9th Army and prepared by Lieutenant Weller. He noted that at 1210 h the Chief-of-Staff of the Luftwaffe 6th Fleet informed the command of the Wehrmacht that: "There are 250 Super Fortresses [sic] with parachutists flying in from the west. Hence the lack of spare fighters."[25]

Soon thereafter, the command of the 9th Army sounded the alarm in a message to the 5th SS Panzer Division Viking, a part of the 9th Army's IV Panzer Corps: "An expected airdrop in the area of Warsaw. Probably paratroopers [will be dropped] over the Kampinos [Forest]."[26]

These few extant German reports demonstrate that news of the American air expedition was spreading rapidly among the units concentrated in the Warsaw area. Thus, the surprise effect was clearly lacking. Most likely the German units began preparations to repulse the attack soon after receiving this message.

As the next dozen or so minutes showed, the moment the expedition passed over the atmospheric front was of great significance for the mission. The circumstances forced the formation to ascend and descend in the vicinity of the designated Initial Point (IP), causing the mission's constituent groups to become dispersed.[27] Thus, confusion began to reign right before the IP, which hindered the mission's success.

Division A, part of the 95th Bomber Group which had been leading the expedition, passed its designated IP, located near Nasielsk (52 36 N, 20 50 E), at 1235 h. The crew piloting the Pathfinder fired a flare to visually confirm the location of the IP and, due to accurate tracking fire, initiated a series of evasive actions.[28] Divisions B and C following in A's stead also began to zigzag and continued to do so until reaching the objective.[29]

The divisions of the 100th Bomber Group entered the bombing path in the areas of Płońsk (Division C, 52 41 N, 20 25 E) and Nasielsk (Division A, 52 37 N, 20 47 E). As a result of earlier maneuvers, the 100th Bomber Group's Division A found itself, at one moment, in front of the lead 95th Bomber Group, and was thereby forced to perform another turn to return to its rightful place in the formation.

Unfortunately, after performing the maneuver the division found itself on the left of the formation. In their report, the commanding navigator, Capt. William J. Dishion Jr., and the lead navigator of the 100th Group, Lt. Ray N. Miller, noted:

> Our group was forced by another group to fly around the IP and, when we turned toward the objective at 1236 h, 52 37 N, 20 47 E, we found ourselves above the front lines and at the receiving end of moderate Flak fire. The speed of the wind, which blew in the direction of 272° was calculated before the IP and was 22 knots, was used by the bombardier to calculate the proper drop point. Intensive evasive action was used before and above the objective during the airdrop at 1245 h on a 170° course and an altitude of 17,000 ft.

Captain John J. Clark, the lead navigator of Division A of the 390th Bomber Group, stated in his after-action report that "The flight unfolded according to plan, excluding the IP, where the weather and the direction in which the parachutes fell forced us to fly past the designated IP, taking a north-south bombing course."[30]

Lieutenant Fletcher F. Conn, the lead bombardier of Division A, reported that "The designated IP was not used by us because it was necessary to fly towards the objective behind a group in front us. Because the designated IP was not used, our course toward the objective ran toward the front line to the north of Warsaw, which forced us to employ sudden evasive action all along the bombing path."[31]

Lieutenant Charles C. Nielsen, the lead bombardier of Division B, noted that:

> Before the IP we had extreme difficulties with the weather, as a result of which when we embarked upon our path we did not turn above it. The anti-aircraft artillery became active before we reached the IP and we were under fire for about 20 min. After entering the bombing path I opened the bomb hatch. As soon as the bomb hatch was opened, our group was attacked by about twenty Me 109s. Our plane came under attack six individual times, and our gunners shot down two of the attacking planes. Evasive action was used up until the R.P.[32]

As Lt. John B. Wey, the lead navigator of Division B, recalled:

> We reached the IP while remaining on course, after which, for whatever reason, we turned to the left and headed to the north of the designated course. When we finally returned to our bombing path we were to the left of the [planned] course

on a 174° path. At the IP our division and the lowest division were attacked by fighters (Me 109s), and our group was seriously dispersed. We continued to fly on course toward the objective, in spite of intensive and accurate Flak fire, and [eventually] conducted the airdrop at 1245 h.

Lieutenant Francis T. Verfurth, the lead navigator of Division C, reported that "The IP was under fire when we were forced to make room for another group. The course was changed to intercept the Bomb release line … Flak anti-aircraft artillery on the bombing path was intensive and accurate."[33]

Lieutenant Gerald H. Farris, the lead bombardier of Division C, remembered:

> When we flew over the IP the navigator gave the pilot an OK signal to turn, but the pilot replied that we are too close to the group in front of us, which was why we have to fly several minutes past the IP. A flare was fired and we turned to enter the bombing path. The bomb hatch was opened at 1231 h.[34]

According to another report, the 390th Bomber Group could not identify its designated IP. In a report submitted in the wake of a completed mission, the commanders of the individual divisions of this group recalled that it was difficult to locate. Division A, which passed the IP by 7–10 miles, found it only after returning. Division C, which passed the IP by 10–15 miles, was forced to continue along the line of the River Vistula. In the same report, the commander of Division B, Maj. Bernard Campbell, stated that following the planned course would have allowed the expedition to avoid the enemy's anti-aircraft barrage.[35]

★★★

As the air armada's leading bombers were approaching Warsaw at 1230 h, several small groups of German Me 109s were spotted by American pilots. The enemy fighters were 10 miles northwest of the city. They were elements of the 6th Air Fleet from Modlin as well as the airfield of Kroczewo to the north of Zakroczym.[36] To conserve fuel supplies, each American squadron only sent only a portion of its fighters to engage and repulse the enemy. The P-51s peeled out of their formation and went after the enemy.

The two opposing forces closed the distance rapidly, and an air battle broke out over the area of Szczytno–Zakroczym–Nasielsk between the Mustangs of the 355th Fighter Group and the 40 German aircraft of the Luftwaffe 6th Fleet.

One of the first to notice the German fighters sneaking up on the rear of the Allied expedition was Lt. Henry W. "Babby" Brown of the "Borax" Squadron.[37] After securing the commander's permission, he turned around to shoot down one Me 109 and damage another. While pursuing two other such aircraft, Lieutenant Brown attacked a well-equipped enemy airfield north of Warsaw, having spotted over 30 Me 109s, Fw 190s, and Ju 87s on its premises. Brown damaged one Junkers Ju 87 Stuka dive bomber and strafed a truck carrying troops. Lieutenant Brown returned to his squadron only right before it completed its escort duties. According to American sources, the Nazis lost four Bf 109 planes while three other German aircraft were damaged.[38]

According to German sources, the American expedition, consisting of 100 "Flying Fortresses" and approximately 50 Mustang fighters, was overtaken and attacked from the front by 28 Bf 109 fighters of the I and IV Squadrons of the 51st Fighter (Pursuit) Regiment "Mölders."[39] According to the authors, during this fight, each German fighter had American fighters on its tail, which gave the Americans a decisive advantage. The American counter-attack dispersed the German foray. Some of the damaged German aircraft were forced to land outside of the airfield, in completely random locations. Due solely to the fact that the Americans broke off the pursuit to reassemble around the bombers they were escorting did the 51st Regiment lose only two airmen.[40] The fight cost the lives of platoon leaders Heinz Junge and Walter Weber, who perished as their aircraft turned over during emergency landing attempts.

Viktor Kittel, a 21-year-old German pilot in 1944, remembered the dogfights of September 18:

> I was an NCO attached to the staff of the commander of the 4th Division of the 51st Fighter Regiment. Very early, on September 18, 1944, we were placed on alert and prepared for a major operation. We expected the raid of at least one-hundred "Flying Fortresses" from the north. Until then, because we had only fought on the Eastern Front, we were only familiar with individual dogfights or, at most, [fights] with squadron-strength units (12 machines). Operations in large formations against

huge bomber formations, which took place during the defense of the Reich, were unfamiliar to us. Hence, we were briefed prior to the operation to attack using an entire division (over 40 fighters) and to stick together. ... My 4th Division took off from Modlin and the 1st Division from Kroczewo. The mechanics had attached additional 300-l fuel tanks to our machines (all were Bf (Me) 109 G6s).

Initially, everything proceeded smoothly. Following orders, both divisions formed two formations and climbed towards the bombers to an altitude of, I believe, 6,000 m.

Approximately around Grudziądz we saw the enemy formations, which were flying at a lower altitude, however. At the beginning we did indeed stick together, but, once we found ourselves close enough to attack nothing could restrain us. We all threw ourselves at the bombers in groups of four machines. Some of the attacking planes in the lead were even able to shoot down a few [bombers]. The others, including myself, were not so lucky, however. Before we could approach closer, we were attacked by droves of American fighters descending from a higher altitude, which had been escorting the bombers. Initially, in the heat of the battle, we completely forgot about them! Dogfights between the fighters of both sides began, causing our formations to be dispersed. Even though we had 80 machines, the Americans had even more fighters. These were Mustangs, Thunderbolts, and Lightning-type planes. We were suddenly transformed from predatory cats into fleeing mice. Only after several hours did we slowly return to our home airbase after most of us were forced to land on some other airfield along the way. While flying along the Vistula river bed I myself ran into two Thunderbolts, which I was able to lose only around the area of Płońsk. I was forced to land there to refuel before returning to my home base.

I am unable to determine whether the 1st Division from Kroczewo suffered losses, or the scale of these losses. My 4th Division lost NCO Junge from the 14th Squadron.[41]

The post-mission reports prepared by the pilots of the 355th Fighter Group claim that among the attacking Germans the greatest aggression and experience was demonstrated by the commanders of the enemy formations. The remaining German pilots were judged as inexperienced and their actions as lacking in vigor.

The Americans lost two fighters, last seen in the pursuit, which belonged to the 358th Squadron of the 355th Fighter Group. Lieutenant Robert O. Peters, born on September 13, 1923, in Bexley, Ohio, was in his 50th combat mission. An experienced pilot, he had once scored five victories (three in the air, two on the ground) on one day, July 20, 1944.

His wingman was Lt. Joseph J. Vigna, born on May 2, 1920, in Sonoma, California. Vigna was participating in his 24th combat mission.[42] A pair was the basic fighter formation in the U.S. Air Force as well, and consisted of a leader and his wingman. During combat, the wingman's main task was to shield the lead fighter, which was to shoot down enemy aircraft. Both Peters and Vigna lost their lives in the aerial combat that day.

According to the testimony of an inhabitant of the village of Kątne near Nasielsk at the time, Wojciech Szabłowski (who was 9 years old in 1944), both the armored column moving along the Nowe Miasto–Nasielsk road, and the Germans stationed in the area, must have been aware of the approaching expedition.[43] Shortly before the appearance of the bombers, a column consisting of tanks and cars turned off the main road in the direction of the village of Kątne. The Germans quickly dispersed their vehicles in the area and camouflaged them as much as possible.

The witness recalls that the American aircraft approaching from the northwest dropped strips of aluminum foil. Known as "Window," these were thin strips of tinfoil used to disrupt German radar. This multiplied the number of objects in the air, which appeared as thousands on the radar screen, off of which the radar waves bounced. This made it very difficult to locate the target, which greatly complicated the aim of anti-aircraft batteries. Soon afterward, the bombers, which had been carefully observed by the Germans who, initially, mistook them for British planes, were subjected to Flak fire from the area of Modlin.

Polish eyewitnesses, interviewed by the Polish Red Cross in 1946, recalled that one of the two American fighters lost on 18 September, a Mustang flown by Lieutenant Vigna, was shot down in a dogfight with three German planes. The pilot bailed out of the burning aircraft in the area on the border of the villages of Kątne and Wymysły.[44] Unfortunately, due to the low altitude from which he jumped, Vigna's parachute failed to deploy in time and he died instantly on hitting the ground.

Szabłowski, who observed the incident, recalls seeing an American fighter incoming from the northeast. The plane initially descended, flying just above the trees in the fields, turned to the right, after which it turned onto its left wing, struck the ground, and exploded. The force of the explosion dispersed its parts over a large area. One could also hear the cracks of the exploding ammunition when the wreck was engulfed in flames. Almost immediately, the German soldiers stationed nearby ran to the site of the crash.

Only the tail section of the plane, along with the tail fins, and the cockpit fairing, which had most likely been cast farther away from the wreck by the force of the explosion, remained. Another American fighter also circled and observed the burning carcass of the plane for a moment. Soon, it departed toward Warsaw, no doubt rushing to catch up with the expedition.

The same witness recalled that some time afterwards a German pilot, most likely the culprit of the kill, arrived at the crash site, probably from the nearby airfield in Chrcynno. Because he made his way through the fields, rather than the road running through Kątne, the witness believed that the field vehicle carrying the German soldiers was most likely following the column of smoke visible from the Nasielsk–Nowe Miasto road.

Wojciech Szabłowski remembered that the dead pilot had sustained serious head wounds and lay supine near the parachute, which had not opened completely. Stanisław Maciątek recalled that, as far as he was aware, the pilot fell out of his cockpit only at the moment of the crash.[45] The Germans wrapped the corpse in paper tarps in a grave they prepared at the crash site. A cross was placed at the head of the grave and a salute volley was fired at the moment of the burial.

Two German documents, marked with the symbols KU 3088 and J 2190, found after the war's end, which most likely originated in the facility for interrogating Allied airmen (Auswertestelle West in Oberursel) state that Vigna's plane crashed in the area of Modlin.[46] He also states that the pilot's dog tags were seized by the German soldiers.

In one of the two documents accompanying the objects located at the crash site, the intelligence department of the 2nd Army's High Command sent the following message to the command of the 6th Air Fleet on September 21, 1944:

> We are enclosing a few documents and items from an American Mustang plane shot down on September 18, 1944 near Kątne X0 1 d (0345).[47] The aircraft is completely destroyed. The pilot is dead next to the plane. (Name: Joseph Vigna).

One handkerchief emblazoned with maps (France, Spain) and a handkit with a metal saw, rope, and tablets. These are still in the office, as permitted by the Head Commander, and will be sent tomorrow.[48]

In the case of the other killed fighter pilot, a clue to establishing the circumstances and place of his death is provided by a report prepared on September 23, 1944. Its introduction described the conditions on September 18 in a laconic but quite interesting manner: altitude, 20,000 ft; time, 1230 h; location, northwest of Warsaw; visibility, poor. Another part of the report also cites the testimony of Lt. Robert M. Thompson of the 355th Fighter Group:

> During our mission to Russia our group was attacked by a dozen enemy planes. Lt. Frost and I attacked two Me 109s, fighting them near Warsaw. Lt. Frost broke off the pursuit due to a problem with his gun sights. During the attack on the enemy aircraft I was joined by a P51 model D. I believe it was Lt. Peters. We flew separately, and I continued pursuing the enemy plane. At this time I saw what I am convinced was the crash of a P51. This could have been the plane of Lt. Peters or Lt. Vigna crashing in a field.[49]

With the benefit of hindsight, it is possible to connect Thompson's report with Lt. Peters, but it is difficult to understand why the map supplementing the account indicated the area of Łowicz as the crash site.

In reality, Lieutenant Peters was shot down about 15 km to the west of Lieutenant Vigna's crash site. According to the testimony of the commander of the 355th Fighter Group, Major Marshall, his plane could have been sandwiched in between two dueling fighters and succumbed to friendly fire from another Mustang of the 358th Squadron which was chasing a German fighter.[50]

Ryszard Wiśniewski, 14 at the time, was an eyewitness. When the air armada appeared, Wiśniewski and his father were near Naruszewka Creek running through the locality of Stara Wrona. The sudden noise caused both men to look up and notice a great number of planes. Below the bombers they also saw the escorting fighters locked in a struggle with German planes, which had taken off from the nearby airfield in Kroczewo. The dogfights occurred above the village. The rattle of machine guns could be heard all around. Suddenly, one of the

American fighters incoming from the northwest tipped over to the side and began to belch smoke. The plane, watched by the onlookers, flew over the creek. Directly above it, the pilot tossed out a map which fell into the water. The locals' attempt to fish it out was unsuccessful. Soon afterward, the smoking aircraft cut across the road linking Przyborowice Górne Dworskie with Stara Wrona.

As the witness recalled, many German troops were deployed in the area at the time. The staff of one of the German units was located in the presbytery building next to the local church. Seeing the smoking, falling plane, the soldiers jumped into their vehicles and, driving on the road between Stara Wrona and Nowa Wrona, followed the aircraft. The downed fighter soon crashed in a cultivated field near the road and a short distance from the local cemetery.

After reaching the crash site, Wiśniewski thought that the pilot most likely attempted to perform an emergency landing since the plane's landing gear was extended, causing the wheels and, as a consequence, the nose, to dig into the ground.

The German soldiers soon surrounded the aircraft and chased them away from the machine, while allowing them to look on from a certain distance. Thus, the witness standing among the crowd could see the pilot sitting in the cockpit. The crowd waved at him, urging him to escape from the aircraft, whose entire tail was now on fire. The pilot, however, only waved back in a gesture of resignation. Soon, the cockpit became filled with smoke through which it was only possible to glimpse the pilot's immobilized silhouette.

According to the testimony, the burning plane did not explode. No sounds of exploding ammunition were to be heard. The fuselage, along with the pilot inside the cockpit, were completely consumed by flames. Only the wings and the wheels remained intact, while the remainder turned into a mix of burned and molten aluminum. When the flames subsided the Germans extracted the remains of the pilot.[51] Peters' body was wrapped in a green tarp (a standard item of a German soldier's equipment). The corpse was then placed into a ditch dug several dozen meters away from the charred wreck. The grave, whose only initial distinguishing feature was a slight depression as compared to the undisturbed soil around, was later marked by the owner of the field by four wooden pegs (one in every corner) to save it from destruction.

The remaining fragments of the plane were later removed from the field by one of the villagers after securing the permission of the Germans. The pieces of sheet metal and the wheels would end up lying near his farmyard for quite a long time.

Probably at a later time, the pilot's remains were moved from the field to the nearby cemetery where, until another exhumation, they were buried next to the mass grave for unknown Polish soldiers who perished in 1920 during the Polish–Soviet War.

Having tied down the escorting fighters with dogfights, in the vicinity of the designated IP near Nasielsk, the German fighters struck at the 390th Bomber Group flying in the rear of the expedition. The group's bombers were assailed by a large number of enemy aircraft which had been initially hiding in the clouds.[52] From among the attackers, eight, or, as another report states, 12, Me 109s and two Fw 190s managed to break through the shield of escorting fighters. At 1230 h, or between 1237 and 1248 h, the German aircraft attacked the group's Division B.

The report, prepared several days afterward, offers a dynamic description of the fighting. The eight previously mentioned Me 109s attacked the leading squadron (A) from the top and rear. After a short skirmish, during which two fighters were destroyed, they became dispersed and simultaneously attacked the lowest squadron (C). At the same time, two other Fw 190s struck at the highest squadron (B), after which they joined the surviving six Me 109s. Next, the remaining four Me 109s (two other Messerschmitts were destroyed by the lower C squadron) began their ascent to attack the highest squadron (B). Here another German aircraft was certainly destroyed and another one probably shot down. After the attack, the enemy planes once again hid in the clouds.

The reports of the 390th Bomber Group indicated that no special markings or painting techniques could be seen on the attacking aircraft. The tactics employed by the Germans were described as traditional and dominated by "roller coaster" or "sneak" type attacks.[53]

During the fight one of the first aircraft to suffer serious damage was a B-17G "Mission Mississippi" (568th Squadron, 390th Bomber

Group) commanded by 2nd Lt. Gerald W. Johnston, whose controls were destroyed by an Fw 190. As Johnston barely managed to fly the aircraft, it was forced to leave the formation. Escorted by four fighters called up to help, it landed in Brześc Litewski, i.e., one of the two Soviet-held airfields (along with Siedlce) designated at the briefing.

The next victim of enemy fighters (apparently, as the report states, 15 of them) was the bomber "Bugs Bunny" (568th Squadron, 390th Bomber Group), which was flying in the second position in the uppermost Division B. Ten minutes before the bomber reached its objective, a 20 mm shell from an Me 109 fighter cannon struck the cockpit and exploded, wounding the plane's commander, Lt. Paul R. Hibbard, and the navigator, Lt. Jack P. Stovall. A part of the control panel was destroyed, the mechanism delivering power to the flaps ceased to function, and the cockpit itself began to burn.

As the second pilot, Lt. James R. O'Neil, later recalled in an article published in the London edition of the daily newspaper of the American Armed Forces, *The Stars and Stripes*, he did not at first notice that his commander suffered wounds. Nothing seemed to indicate it, for, immediately after the cockpit was hit, Lieutenant Hibbard grabbed the fire extinguisher and attempted to snuff out the fire. Eventually, the flames were extinguished by Sergeant Raymond C. Foppiano, who was in charge of the bow turret and risked his life to assist the second pilot who called on him to help.

Meanwhile, the navigator, Lieutenant Stovall, lost consciousness for a period of almost 2 h. Bomb-aimer Sergeant Jack G. Edwards was also wounded while helping his comrades. In spite of the immediate assistance provided by the second pilot and the bomb–aimer, Lieutenant Hibbard died as a result of a serious left leg wound before the crew managed to drop supplies and reach the base.

After departing the airdrop area the damaged aircraft found itself 10 miles behind the main formation. Seeing the damaged bomber isolated, enemy fighters swarmed in and attacked it once more. During this assault a 20 mm shell struck the arm, face, and right hand of the tail gunner, Sergeant Robert E. Underwood. But Underwood managed to return to his position and shoot down one of the attacking fighters, in spite of serious bleeding from the mouth. The sergeant remained at his post until the pain became unbearable. Later, while searching for help, he reached the positions of the side gunners. Here the radio operator, who served as the onboard medic, Lester H. Baumgarte, dressed his wounds. Private William L. Fletcher took over Underwood's post and destroyed another enemy plane.

The extant testimonies indicate that most of the expedition's participants remembered the dramatic radio communiqué uttered by the second pilot, O'Neil, who contacted the commander of Division B, Major Campbell, soon after departing from the Rally Point: "My pilot has been hit, my navigator is wounded. Another man is wounded in the tail of the plane, it is very difficult for me to control the plane. What should I do?" Major Campbell attempted to calm him by providing the only available counsel: "We will slow down as much as possible. There is not much you can do. Stay close to us. That is your only hope."[54]

The aircraft continued its flight in spite of severe problems: a damaged left elevator, rudder, and left inner engine turbocharger; the destruction of half of the control panel, including the speedometer; and inoperative flaps. Sergeant Harold B. Blumberg, the commander of the ground-based mechanics who flew as part of the air crew who also served as the right side gunner, managed to perform some makeshift maintenance work, allowing the aircraft to reach Mirgorod safely.[55]

The report submitted after the mission emphasized Sergeant Blumberg's dedication. With no regard for his safety, no parachute, and an open bomb chamber, he managed to repair the rudder cables by utilizing only a pair of tweezers and a heating cable from a flight suit. In addition, Blumberg shot down an enemy plane while operating both the left- and right-side machine guns.

After a brush with the enemy fighters, yet another aircraft was forced from its formation. Piloted by Lt. Fidel G. Galetti, the B 17G "Songon" (571st Squadron, 390th Bomber Group), lost altitude and was repeatedly attacked by the German planes. The pilots took to evasive actions, as the gunners defended the plane, managing to keep the enemy at a safe distance. Thanks to these actions, the bomber eventually reached its destination.

According to American sources, the determined gunners of the 390th Bomber Group shot down eight aircraft confirmed, in addition to three more probable kills, and one more damaged enemy plane, during this mission.[56]

A former member of Lieutenant Akins' crew, the tail gunner Platoon Leader Vincent J. Stefanek, also witnessed the aerial combat that day.[57] Stefanek was on board the B-17 G "I'll Get By" (568th Squadron of the 390th Bomber Group, pilot: Lt. Carl B. Mazzuchelli).[58] Stefanek recalled that the German fighters came from the geographic position of 52 36 N—20 50 (a point east of Nasielsk) at an altitude of 15,000 ft at 1237 h. The attacking aircraft, which struck from above at 5:30 (1730 h), was shot down by him and the top gunner, Senior Sergeant John R. McCaw. Meanwhile, the bottom gunner, Sergeant Robert E. Daigle, also fired at the enemy plane. The official record states:

> The Me 109s were flying from a 9 o'clock position in a direction opposite to ours and were outside of the range of our fire. Behind the formation the planes performed a 180° turn at 5:30. As soon as one of the enemy planes found itself within firing range he approached and opened fire from the guns in his wings from a distance of about 500 yards. The top and tail gunners opened fire from 300 to 600 yards. They fired in short volleys, adjusting their aim throughout to take account of the lead aircraft. At a distance of about 400 yards the enemy aircraft began to burn. It approached to a distance of 75 yards and flipped over. The plane was burning from nose to tail. Next the enemy aircraft spun out of control and fell toward the ground. As soon as the first aircraft began to burn the second one fled to the left. No parachutes were seen.[59]

CHAPTER 4

Airdrop

On September 18, 1944, approximately 2 h before noon, Polish insurgent units in Warsaw received word of an expected airdrop. They were ordered to prepare observation posts on rooftops and to man the city squares and streets. The arrival of the air armada less than 3 h later caused euphoria among the civilians and the insurgents. Everyone who was in the city or its vicinity on that day remembered it well.

The famous Polish-Jewish pianist, Władysław Szpilman, who was hiding from the Germans in the area of Aleja Niepodległości (Independence Avenue), recalled: "On September 18 airplanes appeared which dropped supplies over the city for the insurgents. I saw the parachutes, but I did not see whether these were people or weapons."[1]

Exhausted and often wounded people hiding in the cellars ventured into the city streets. Intrigued, they climbed atop the rubble heaps or the rooftops to discover the source of the growing and vibrating noise and to observe the expected developments from a closer vantage point. When the bombers appeared in the air, many inhabitants waved to the passing aircraft, and others cried out joyously and cheered. Many witnesses recalled that it was at this very moment that they felt that the long-awaited help was finally arriving. After a long and lonely struggle, accompanied by a growing feeling of hopelessness, they finally came to believe that they had not been forgotten and that their voice had reached the Allies.

When parachutes eventually appeared in the sky, the crowds' reaction became even more enthusiastic. Paying no attention to possible wounds caused by shrapnel produced by the frenzied German anti-aircraft defense, many Varsovians embraced or hugged one another, crying and giving vent to their pent-up emotions. Some laughed nervously. Some believed that the falling containers were actually paratroopers, thinking that they were witnessing the long-awaited assault of General Sosabowski's airborne brigade.

> Whoever was alive ran out into the street. A frenzy of joy overwhelmed the city. I witnessed people who had never known each other embracing one another. A wounded man with a crutch was jumping on one leg while holding on to another random passerby's neck. Applause, applause, teary eyes, [and] feverish faces.[2]

The testimony of the Main Commander of the Home Army contained in his memoir, *Armia Podziemna*, shines a light on the expedition as it was awaited and observed:

> We were awaiting with great impatience the American air expedition, which had been announced so many times, but called off just as often due to atmospheric conditions. Finally, on the night of September 17 to 18, the BBC announced the expedition.
>
> We awaited the morning [radio] program with great anticipation. If it is followed by the song "One More Mazur Today" [*"Jeszcze jeden mazur dzisiaj"*], the expedition will take off. If the song is "The March of the Infantry" [*"Marsz Piechoty"*], then we will be disappointed once again.
>
> This time "One More Mazur Today" followed the program. Immediately afterwards, we received a dispatch to expect the expedition between 11 and 12 noon.
>
> It was a nice, sunny day. Not a cloud in the sky.
>
> The denizens of Warsaw knew nothing of the impending expedition, of course, so the sight of incoming American planes which suddenly appeared above the city generated indescribable joy.
>
> The bombers flew very high up, leaving behind them an array of white dots. These were the parachutes.
>
> The Germans opened up a hurricane of anti-aircraft artillery fire but it failed to reach the machines.

Warsaw experienced moments of indescribable enthusiasm. All save for the wounded and the sick, left the cellars.

Underground spaces emptied out and the courtyards and streets filled up. At first, we assumed that this was an airborne assault. A soldier standing nearby was observing the sky through his binoculars. Suddenly, he yelled out loudly: "Dear Jesus, the Germans will shoot them all down!"

One of the officers attempted to calm him down by explaining that these were not paratroopers but containers with arms and ammunition. But the soldiers replied that: "But I can see clearly through the binoculars that they are swinging their legs in the air."

The Germans sounding the alarm "Amerikanische Fallschirmjaeger" were probably under the same erroneous impression.

The shells fired by the anti-aircraft artillery kept exploding in the air and the resulting shrapnel would sometimes strike individual parachutes, whose containers would then fall vertically to the ground.

Immediately after being dropped, the parachutes hovered above our lines, but the wind soon swept them further away. The majority of the crates, along with the contents, fell onto streets and houses which had been in our hands a week before, but were now held by the enemy.

When the airplanes departed, the crowds cheered joyously and looked up into the sky for a while longer, only to soon return to their cellars and shelters with heads hung in sadness. The people understood the scale of the assistance they could have received had it come earlier. During the first weeks [of the uprising], when we held two-thirds of the city, about one thousand containers would have undoubtedly fallen into our hands. Had we received such a huge quantity of weapons and ammunition we could have not only liberated Warsaw in its entirety, but we would have held it as well.

Unfortunately, we now held only scraps of the territory we previously captured. Only a tiny number of containers dropped from such an altitude fell within our positions. We witnessed a great demonstration of the power of the Allied air force, a power whose assistance came too late.[3]

The containers dropped by the aircraft fell in different parts of the city. Most witness testimonies come from the northern part of the Warsaw City Center and Northern Mokotów district, the fewest from the southern City Center, Czerniaków, and Żoliborz. The number of witnesses in each area is proportional to the quantity of containers dropped over these parts of Warsaw and the supplies captured. Having been carried by the wind, the containers sometimes fell in areas held by the insurgents. At other times, to their great despair, the cargo landed in territory held by the Germans or in areas adjacent to the frontlines, making it necessary to fight for them.

In the Northern City Center, most of the containers fell in the western part of that district over the positions held by the Home Army's "Chrobry II" Grouping. In the area delineated by Pańska, Sienna, Twarda, and Śliska Streets a total of 34 containers were captured. One fell in the cutting (*wykop*) of the Cross-City Railroad near Żelazna Street; it was soon captured, under enemy fire, by the soldiers of Lt. Zbigniew Brym "Zdunin's" 5th Company holding the Postal Railroad Station (*Dworzec Pocztowy*) Redoubt. The testimony of the unit's commander allows us to sense the atmosphere accompanying operations to capture the airdropped containers.

> We began to … collect the containers in a hurry. The Germans naturally concentrated their fire on our positions and especially the places where the crates supposedly fell. The gathering of these weapons and ammunition for fighting Warsaw, a treasure from the sky, sometimes generated bitter misunderstandings. Sometimes, arguments, rows, and even fighting would erupt. I quickly secured and organized the collection of the containers which fell onto our territory. But often the soldiers proved faster. When a gathering team reached the containers, they were completely gutted. Sometimes only a beautiful nylon canopy indicated the spot where the crate had fallen. Many soldiers, and team and position commanders immediately utilized the weapons on the frontlines. … The enthusiasm was frantic. For it was true that [the airdropped supplies] were a veritable treasure for us. There were machine guns, automatic pistols, all including the proper ammunition, small arms, Smith-Wesson revolvers, and even "Piat" anti-tank weaponry. There were also bandages, medicine, and medical supplies. There were even small quantities of elements for uniforms, and even chocolate and cigarettes.
>
> Smiles, joy, and happiness returned to the soldiers' faces that day. Talks and discussions on this subject, as well as the accompanying praise for the Americans, were endless.[4]

One of the 17 containers captured by the II Battalion of the "Chrobry II" Grouping fell near the "Konrad, Jarnuszkiewicz i S-ka" hospital equipment factory on Grzybowska Street n. 25. Unfortunately, the area was held by the Germans at the time. Despite the opposition of the unit commander, 2nd Lt. Leonard Kancelarczyk "Jaremi," the men undertook the dangerous attempt to recover the crate by utilizing a firehook. The price paid for seizing the container was the death of a young liaison who was killed as a result of the shooting. In the area of Waliców Street, another container was taken by Capt. Wacław Zagórski *nom de guerre* "Lech Grzybowski," who described the moments without disguising his excitement:

> Rysiek, Geniek, and I lunged toward the first container, which had fallen next to the outlet of Walicowa toward the ruins of the Ghetto. Luckily, it was in a giant crater. How easy it was to open the buckles of the metal armor! Inside there were boxes fitted with straps, ready to be carried easily like a backpack. [There were] English machine guns with ready-to-use ammunition belts. ... We returned to the command center. In the entry gate there were two unopened containers which had been dragged from the rubble behind the lumber mill. ... We opened these containers in the entry gate. The first one [held] Stens and ammunition. The second one plastic, mines, detonators, and guns for the sappers. The third one anti-tank weapons: Piats along with the projectiles. The fourth one food: Argentinian canned meat, chocolate, tea biscuits. The fifth one medical. The hands of the nurses were shaking when they removed blood for transfusions. Everything was labeled in Polish. The blood was donated by Poles at the Polish hospital in Edinburgh.[5]

A few other containers were captured by the soldiers of Capt. Wacław Stykowski "Hal's" grouping, which held the buildings of the "Pluton" factory on Grzybowska Street no. 37. Other crates fell in the center of the district and onto the positions held by Major Włodzimierz Zawadzki "Bartkiewicz."

As opposed to the relatively numerous containers captured by the "Chrobry II" unit, only two fell onto the positions held by the adjacent "Gurt" Grouping. One of these was initially gliding above the headquarters of the unit at Chmielna Street no. 103. This moment was captured on a photograph taken by Corporal Jan Żulma "Feliks" of the 3rd Company, 152nd Platoon.

Unfortunately, the container fell onto the side of the Cross-City Railroad cutting between Żelazna Street and the Main Railroad Station.

It was thus within range of German fire. Sharpshooter Kazimierz Styczyński "Strzelec" from the 152nd Platoon volunteered to deliver it. Under the cover of darkness, Styczyński cautiously crawled up to the container, tying to it a rope attached to him. The daring man's brothers-in-arms pulled the end of the rope and dragged the container towards them. To their joy, the insurgents found 10 Sten guns along with cartridges and ammunition, and "Gammon"-type grenades.

The second container landed in "no-man's-land" in front of the positions of the 1st Company and was under fire by the Germans. After darkness descended, both the Germans and the insurgents attempted to pull the container over to their side, but both sides failed.

The rebels feverishly searched for a way to capture the container, but all ideas ended up in failure or proved immediately unviable. Then someone proposed that German prisoners be used to retrieve the containers. The idea was rejected as excessively cruel.

Self-sacrifice was the only way for the soldiers to capture the supplies. Two men volunteered: Infantry Corporal Marian Grzychaczewski "Sygurt" of the 153rd Platoon, and Corporal "Henryk" (probably Platoon Leader/Sergeant Henryk Rycharski of the 153rd Platoon). The volunteers were accepted by the commander of the 1st Company, Capt. Stanisław Tomaszewski "Jednorożec," and were to set out at dawn. The goal was to use a rope, just like in the case of the first container. Right before the action began, the Polish observers monitoring "no-man's-land" reported that the Germans were attempting to grab the container by using Poles they had captured. As they approached the container, the prisoners called out to the insurgents, begging them not to shoot because they had been terrorized into submission by the Germans and had no other choice but to comply. Soon thereafter, four of them seized the container. As it turned out, it contained medical supplies badly required by the insurgents.

Another container fell, struck along its way by tree branches, in "no-man's-land" stretching between the ruins of the Warsaw Stock Exchange and the Orangerie in the Saxon Gardens.[6] The latter was held by the Germans. The mutual war of the nerves lasted until darkness arrived. At about midnight, 2nd Lt. Ignacy Szczeniowski "Paprzyca," along with four volunteers, set out from his command in the ruins of the Królewska Street no. 16 Redoubt (adjacent to the ruins of the Stock Exchange) in the direction of the container. To avoid making noise, the daring men wrapped their boots in rags. They crawled and crept the entire way toward the container. Lieutenant "Paprzyca" cut off the parachute, which had been caught on the tree branches, and left it. The men then succeeded in dragging the container to home base. The crate contained 16 Stens, along with additional cartridges, which the soldiers of the 9th Company of the Kiliński Battalion were allowed to keep as a gesture of recognition.

Ten other containers fell in the area of the Pomological Garden (on the corner of Emilia Plater and Wspólna Streets), in front of the positions of the "Zaremba-Piorun" Battalion. Following heavy fighting by German and Polish patrols, the insurgents managed to capture some of these crates. In the Southern City Center a single container also landed near one of the barricades held in the area of Marszałkowska Street and Savior's Square by the 3rd "Golski" Armored Battalion. Attempts to retrieve it met with an immediate German reaction. Thus, the container was only captured under the cover of night.

In the case of Upper Mokotów, the aircraft arrived from the direction of Ochota district. Witnesses saw multi-colored parachutes fall in the area of the eastern part of Mokotów Field. Most likely the entirety of this airdrop fell into the hands of the Germans from Rakowiecka Street. An unknown number of containers also fell in the area of Odyńca Street, behind the Park of General Orlicz-Dreszer, on Puławska Avenue, and near the positions of the 3rd Company, 1st Battalion, the "Baszta" Regiment. Sometimes, as in other districts, the Poles waited for darkness to arrive to venture out to retrieve the treasure.

As Lesław M. Bartelski recalled, one of the containers airdropped that day fell in the area of a park and a classical palace known as the "Rabbit Hutch," located on a Vistula embankment.[7] He saw Senior Sharpshooter Wojciech Militz "Bystry" from the 3rd "Baszta" Regiment's Company B run:

> ... down the embankment under the cover of an insurgent hand-held machine gun in the direction of a horticultural farm whose owners were already dividing

up the unexpected spoils. Using one silk parachute as a carrot, and the threat of using his weapon as the stick, he managed to reclaim the Bren, along with all the complete equipment and ammunition, and an additional barrel and cartridges. A teenage boy helped the insurgent carry the weaponry and both climbed the escarpment. Meanwhile, the enemy fired at them from afar. Upon reaching the building housing Giżycki's school, "Bystry" cleaned the grease off of the light machine gun and fired off a test burst in the direction of Sobieski Avenue.

The company retained the Bren with the permission of the regimental command.[8]

Only a small number of containers were captured by the men fighting in Upper Czerniaków, although the district was in a very precarious situation. The area delineated by Zagórna, Czerniakowska, Okrąg, and Ludna Streets, as well as Solec and the Vistula, was too small for a precise airdrop.

The insurgents of Żoliborz would be even more disappointed. In the hope of capturing all the airdropped supplies, a patrol commanded by Platoon Leader Kazimierz Kozłowski "Mały" laid out signal tarps on Wilson Square, the center of the area held by the units of the "Żywiciel" insurgent district, before the arrival of the air expedition.

Once the airplanes appeared, the enthusiasm generated by the sight of the parachutes was as great as in the other districts. Inhabitants gazing at the skies with hope filled up the squares and streets here as well. Unfortunately, the parachutes were blown behind the German lines in the direction of Wawrzyszew, Powązki, and Bemowo, most likely as a result of a change in the wind direction. The insurgents in Żoliborz were unable to secure even one container.

On the same day, in his dispatch to Prime Minister Mikołajczyk, the Plenipotentiary of the Government, Jankowski, cabled:

Thank you for today's airdrops. I do not have data as to the contents yet. Some fell into German hands, some into those of the Soviets in Praga [district], but the fact of Allied assistance alone greatly boosted the spirits of the population and the army. People jumped from joy.[9]

The German command in the Warsaw area faced a complex and confusing tactical picture on September 18 . Soviet forces were just across the Vistula, Polish Home Army troops throughout Warsaw and the nearby Kampinos, and now an armada of American aircraft overhead. The

Germans initially assumed that all three Allied forces were engaged in a coordinated operation. The situation report of the German 9th Army from September 18, 1944, dispatched to the command of Army Group Center, associated the movements of the Soviet units invading from the direction of Wołomin and Radzymin, as well as the increased activities of Polish partisan groups in the eastern parts of the Kampinos Forest, with an impending American air expedition, which, the Germans suspected, would drop airborne troops in the area. They expected the three forces to work in unison to destroy the German units concentrated in the Vistula–Narew river fork, which included units forming the 4th SS Panzer Corps. A 9th Army daily report from September 18 stated:

> Right after 1100 h, an insurgent attack was reported from the southeastern part of the Kampinos Forest. Also, at 1100 h a Russian hurricane bombardment began on the southern wing of the 4th SS Panzer Corps. The shortest road to the Kampinos Forest leads through here.

> The danger escalated even more when, about 1 h later, the signal came that 250 American four-engine bombers were approaching, and these [bombers] were, according to a credible source, to airdrop paratroopers in the Warsaw area. Even if it later turned out that, instead of paratroopers, the Allies only dropped supplies, 90% of which fell into our hands, the air raid was nevertheless stunningly coordinated with the Russian attacks. Especially since the American bombers did not drop all of their cargo. Perhaps this happened because the Russian and insurgent attacks did not achieve a breakthrough and their game did not bring about the desired results.

> In case the fighting spreads from the eastern and western direction, the 9th Army will respond immediately by inserting the 2nd Panzer Grenadier Regiment, which was still held in reserve, and formed a part of the Hermann Goering Division, into the southeastern areas of the Kampinos Forest and northwestern Żoliborz.[10]

Another description of the air operation conducted over Warsaw appeared in the daily report of the counterintelligence section of the 9th Army's reconnaissance unit:

> At approximately 1345 h [we observed] 100–120 Anglo-American aircraft fly past, which dropped a large number of containers with supplies in the areas east of Modlin, above Warsaw, and to the west of Warsaw. According to the reports in our possession, we can ascertain that only about 200–250 containers fell into

the insurgents' hands. The crates contained: anti-tank weapons (*panzerschreck*), machine guns, mpi [sic], food, and clothing. Dolls had been tied to some parachutes for the purpose of deception. The parachutes were white, red, and black. Contrary to other reports, it should be assumed that only individual paratroopers were dropped.[11]

The Army Group Center's daily report dispatched at 0015 h on September 19 states that German fighters and anti-aircraft artillery shot down three four-engine planes each.[12] The same document noted that the Flak units of the 19th Panzer Division shot down bombers, and that the 3rd SS "Totenkopf" Panzer Division and the 5th SS "Viking" Panzer Division shot down one four-engine "Flying Fortress" bomber each.

On the same day, at 0720 h, the 9th Army notified the command of Army Group Center:

> Yesterday, the area of Modlin and Warsaw was invaded by about 100 American Fortresses, each of which conducted about 10 drops on a wide front using black, white, red, and green parachutes and dropping crates containing grenade-launchers, machine guns, ammunition, supplies, and clothing. Reports, which are still incomplete, state that it has been possible to capture 250 parachutes with supplies by now. We should expect this number to grow because the parachutes were dropped from high altitudes and were dispersed over a large area.[13]

Similar information may be found in the log kept by the commander of the German forces in Warsaw, SS-Obergruppenführer Erich von dem Bach-Zelewski, who noted with some relief that:

> At noon the alarm was suddenly sounded: several hundred four-engine American bombers were heading our way. Over a thousand parachutes. Luckily, these were only containers which, thanks to the favorable wind, fell mostly into our hands. Only a small part reached the Polish cauldron.[14]

The events transpiring above the city also captured the attention of a German soldier serving in a transport company who was standing guard at the time. Heinrich Stechbarth left a diary that gave a detailed and somewhat ironically painful record illustrating the airdrop. On September 18 Stechbarth wrote in his diary:

> Standing guard at our posts today, we witnessed events that most of us had up to now only seen in newsreels. Around 1355 h, a squadron of American and British planes flying at an altitude of about 1,000 m appeared, initially flying

in formations of two or three machines. There must have been more than fifty (I managed to count only up to forty-four, after which I lost track). There is a whole mass of them up there, as if an entire large group of birds took off. Then we saw that something was falling out of these planes above our heads. The parachutes opened! The alarm was sounded and the artillery began to rumble. Some claimed that they saw the hands and feet of paratroopers. Was this finally an airborne assault like in the West? But this was very unlikely here. The parachutes fell and I saw black, green, and white canopies … Oh, these were containers with supplies! … Others contain German ammunition. How decent these guys are! The Americans are bringing weapons and ammunition, which we hurriedly abandoned in the West, and are delivering it to us here in Warsaw by plane![15]

A report summing up the activities of the 6th German Air Fleet, dated November 16, 1944, states that:

An American supply expedition of September 18 deserves particular attention. A formation of about 150 Fortresses shielded by 60 fighters entered the Warsaw area from the west. After circling in the area of Schröttersburg [Płock] for up to an hour, the formation dropped, from an altitude of 4,000 m, about 1,000 supply containers near Modlin and SO Błonie. About 80% of the entire load, consisting of ammunition, weapons, clothing, and supplies, fell into our hands.

Presumably the supplies were intended for the Kampinos Forest because fire signals could be spotted in that area during the air raid.

Having lost three of their own, the fighters shot-down two Fortresses, lit another on fire [and] most likely forced it to conduct an emergency landing. The Anti-Aircraft Artillery shot down three more Fortresses.[16]

This succinct description indicates that the Germans noticed the formations circling in the area of Płock, most likely related to attempts to overcome the storm front, and that the Polish units deployed in the Kampinos Forest were prepared to intercept the airdrops in the event of an emergency. It also provides more information on the losses suffered by the Luftwaffe, raising the number of German losses from two to three aircraft.

CHAPTER 5

"I'll Be Seeing You"

Only a fraction of the supplies dropped by the ill-fated and politically charged *Frantic 7* mission reached their intended recipients, though compared with other U.S. air missions over occupied Europe, it suffered limited casualties despite encountering heavy anti-aircraft fire and fighter attacks. That was small consolation, however, for the men who were shot down that day and their families. In particular, the loss of one American plane, the B-17 "I'll Be Seeing You" and its crew came to symbolize the fate of the *Frantic 7* operation.

According to American sources, at approximately 1245 h, 4 min prior to reaching the objective, a German fighter attacked Lieutenant Akins' plane.[1] The left horizontal stabilizer became detached and the right internal engine no. 3 caught fire. Members of other crews noticed the falling doors of the tail hatch and also observed that the aircraft, which had been flying at an altitude of 14,000 ft, abandoned its formation, ditched its cargo, and performed a controlled descent to an altitude of 3,000 ft (approximately 900 m) and exploded in the air at approximately 1246 h at that height. Soon, two parachutes were seen falling toward the ground.

German sources indicate that Lieutenant Akins' B-17 was shot down by a fighter, which took off from the airfield at Kroczewo, and was piloted by Lt. Günther Josten, Staffelkapitän of the 3 Staffel I Gruppe Jadgeschwader 51 "Mölders."[2] According to one German report, the bomber was shot down at an altitude of 4,000 m at 1345 h.[3] As we shall see later, in light of other sources, it is difficult to determine the credibility of this information, and it is problematic to assign the kill solely to Lieutenant Josten.

Thanks to the recollections written down in 1986 by the radio operator Technical Sergeant Marcus Shook, one of only two surviving members of Lieutenant Akins' crew, we may familiarize ourselves with the events of September 18, 1944 as Shook remembered them.

> We viewed the flight to Warsaw as a routine one, and I think that the excitement and the sense that something tragic was to happen did not appear before reaching the objective.
>
> Because I was in the loading dock and the bomb bay doors were already open, this must have happened already after reaching the Initial Point. I was standing on the narrow plank running through the middle of the bomb chamber. I did not have my earphones on and wasn't aware of what was going on outside until "Gizmo" [Frank De Cillis] came down from his top turret and called me into the radio operator's space while pointing at the right wing. Because he did not go with me, I thought that he therefore went for his parachute. I went back, looked through the window, and saw fire. The right internal engine was burning and the flames were slowly creeping towards the fuel tank.[4] I immediately threw down my anti-shrapnel jacket, put on a chest parachute, and headed for the exit. There, I think, I saw George [Mac Phee] leaving his bubble [the bottom turret] and heading for the exit. There was no panic among us, and Paul [Haney], me, and James [Christy] lined up to bail out of the plane in that order through the emergency exit.[5]
>
> The flames were burning all along the fuselage and were already licking the door, which, I believe, caused our hesitation whether to jump. Suddenly, the plane performed a 90° turn onto its wing, which pushed us to the right side of the fuselage. Then, equally suddenly, Francis [Akins] and "Doc" [Shaw] returned the plane back to equilibrium. This sudden maneuver thrust us to the other side causing us all to fall to the floor while crawling toward the exit.
>
> I'm sure that I bailed out of the plane first. Did Paul [Haney] cross himself? I thought that as soon as I jumped, an explosion sealed the fate of everyone else who didn't.
>
> I know that during the explosion I reflexively pulled the cord which released the canopy and the force of the opening parachute caused me to pass out. I have no idea how long I was unconscious. I remember thinking I was dead. I decided to see what time I passed out and, when I raised my left hand toward my face, my

watch showed 12:35. At that time I realized that I wasn't dead and I began to survey the ground below me. Far below I noticed a white parachute canopy. I don't know whose parachute that could have been.

Although I saw the explosion which ripped off the right wing, I don't remember seeing the plane hitting the ground.[6]

In a facsimile of Shook's letter, dated August 1, 1945, fragments of which survived and were quoted in an archival document addressed to an unknown individual, he wrote that the bomber was attacked by an Fw 190 and an Me 109. As a result, engine no. 3 was engulfed in flames. The damaged aircraft was forced to abandon its formation, making it the object of further enemy fighter attacks.

These dramatic events were described by Polish eyewitness Klemens Bogurat, 20 years old at the time, who was a forced laborer conscripted to build a road running through the meadows between Dziekanów Polski and Kiełpin, leading to the temporary crossing of the Vistula River. Bogurat recalled:

Our attention was first captured by the noise of approaching airplanes. Soon thereafter a few fighters scouting the ground appeared. The escalating humming of the grouped bombers caused us to stop work and begin observing the unfolding events while sitting under the trees.

The appearance of so many bombers provoked an immediate reaction from four nearby anti-aircraft guns, whose crews began to feverishly fire on the mass of aircraft flying above.

A bomber which I noticed soon afterwards was struck in the tail, which caused the part to break off. The machine continued on its course in spite of this. Its crew ditched the cargo the plane had been transporting.

The sight of falling containers caused a crazed reaction on the part of the Germans, who probably mistook them as paratroopers and began to strafe them with small arms.[7]

According to the witness, amongst the numerous parachutes, to which containers were attached, there was no possibility of recognizing any of the members of the crew bailing out from the plane. The large number of parachutes mentioned in this testimony leads one to assume that other planes also conducted drops in the area of Dziekanów Polski in addition to the cargo ditched by Lieutenant Akins' plane as an emergency measure.[8]

Thirteen-year-old Edward Figauzer also witnessed the shooting down of the bomber. Forced by the Germans to abandon his home on September 18, he was staying with his family on the right side of the Vistula in a village in the area of Kępa Tarchomińska. It was from this vantage point that he observed the events in question. The unusually large flight consisting of four-engine aircraft made a huge impression on him. As he observed, the American planes followed the line of the Vistula on its opposite side. Due to the decades that have elapsed since, Figauzer does not remember if the bombers were accompanied by fighters. In his assessment, however, the fighters could well have been flying above the bombers.

Looking in the direction of fighting Warsaw, Figauzer noticed an airdrop, which was conducted in advance of reaching the city. The parachutes were then carried by the wind and drifted toward the Kampinos Forest, provoking a barrage of fire from a diverse array of weapons. Individual German soldiers from various panzer units, who were stationed close to the witness, were clearly confused. Unaware of whether they faced a supply drop or an airborne assault, they fired at the distant planes using whatever arms were at their disposal, including machine pistols. Given the vast distance separating these Germans from the aircraft, this behavior seemed irrational even to the then 13-year-old boy.

At this point, Figauzer noticed a bomber that had its wings and engines break off as a result of a hit by an anti-aircraft shell. The wings fell to the ground much faster than the fuselage itself, which attracted the boy's attention with the fact that it was engulfed by flames on one side and descended slowly while turning on its axis.

Zygmunt Skarbek-Kruszewski's personal memoirs, constituting part of the anthology titled *Bellum Vobiscum War Memoirs*, also offer both an interesting and detailed description of the events of September 18.[9] Employed as a laborer on the premises of Modlin airfield at the time, Skarbek-Kruszewski wrote:

> Suddenly, someone pointed in the direction of the western horizon. In the sky we could see a large number of shiny points flying in a big formation. ... Shortly

thereafter, other formations appeared in the sky. Until that point, the entire air was buzzing to the noise of strong monotone vibrations. ... Suddenly, our airfield came to life. The alarm was sounded. Some German planes took off to leave the airfield in a great hurry. The pilots ran towards their planes. Meanwhile, the first [Allied] squadron was already approaching the airfield. They [the Allied bombers] flew majestically; they looked huge. Their large aluminum wings glittered in the sun. They appeared like flying tanks. They were the four-engine American Fortresses. The German anti-aircraft artillery opened fire. Now the air vibrated even more due to the tumult of the heavy guns. A hail of small shrapnel fell in the sand near the bunker, as if someone had thrust a handful of stones into the sand. Anyone who could escape from the airfield did so. We only had sufficient time to jump into an unfinished trench in which we hugged its sides. "This will be our end," said someone, as if to console us. "The Americans don't joke around." Full of anxiety, we awaited the first bombs. But the first squadron passed by above us. Wave after wave, they bypassed and continued eastward.

In spite of the fact that the German artillery continued to fire at the air expedition, the men hiding in the trench wished to witness the unfolding events. They peeked out from their makeshift shelter and observed that:

The entire sky was covered with small white clouds produced by the exploding shells. The aircraft were flying majestically above and through them [the explosions] while keeping the designated distance between one another. They flew calmly, evenly, and slowly, like the departing cranes during the fall. ... Our emotions reached their zenith when we saw what was happening. The planes, which crossed the Vistula, began dropping small white dots, which opened up like large umbrellas.

"Parachutes!" the people yelled out while laughing and jumping on the grass. "The Americans have come to help us." The joy was indescribable. ... At the airfield the Germans sounded the alarm against the [alleged] paratroopers. The men put on their helmets, ammunition belts, and grabbed their automatic rifles. Armored cars full of armed soldiers drove through the field. Motorcycles rode through in a hurry. This was a total emergency. The minutes passed and the planes disappeared behind the horizon. The firing ceased and the parachutes disappeared from the line of sight behind the Vistula. The alarm was called off and we were ordered to return to work.

Ryszard Szcześniak, a wartime resident of Dziekanów Polski, was a 12-year-old boy at the time.[10] Like all the other villagers, he observed the majestic air armada above with great curiosity. He recalled:

It was a sunny day with good visibility and the never-before seen mass of low-flying aircraft and the din of their engines made a stunning and unforgettable impression. The Germans stationed in the village of Dziekanów Polski, who feared an assault by American paratroopers, panicked. The impression of generalized chaos, prevailing both on the ground and in the air, was exacerbated by intense anti-aircraft artillery fire. These guns were deployed in the meadows near the Vistula River crossing in Dziekanów Polski.

The airplanes dropped at least several dozen containers in the area, and a few of them fell into a nearby lake. The damaged aircraft crashed in the fields between the Warsaw–Modlin road and the buildings of Dziekanów Niemiecki.

According to the same testimony, the plane did not explode at the moment of impact. Its nose pointed in the direction of Warsaw, while the wreckage, when observed from afar, appeared to be whole.

After the war, James Christy stated that the enemy fighter attacked their bomber around 1335 h. Just prior to this, he noticed a fragment from another unidentified machine in the air. As a result of the attack, the right wing went up in flames. Upon bailing out and looking up, he noted that the aircraft continued to fly. While descending, he did not see any other crew members, nor did he observe the explosion or the moment of impact.

In another report on the fate of the individual crew members submitted after the war, Christy mentioned that he bailed out of the plane at 1320 h by crawling out of the tail hatch.[11] Before jumping, he saw Shook and Haney on the floor. He also testified that he was not aware of whether the other crew members bailed out. He was only certain as to the radio operator, Shook. He also stated that, earlier on, during a conversation over the intercom, the onboard gunner, Sergeant Haney, said that he had shot down one Me 109. However, the connection was soon lost and, soon thereafter, the entire communication system in the plane ceased functioning. He remembered that the falling aircraft was burning violently and appeared completely inoperative. Because of the cloud cover, he did not see the moment of impact itself.

The same report noted that radio operator Shook saw Senior Sergeant De Cillis when he was heading in his direction through the bomb chamber holding a fire extinguisher. Apparently, he wished to check out the situation or hoped that he could extinguish the flames, but Shook turned him back and pointed toward the burning engine no. 3. As to his ability to bail out of the plane, he stated that the top turret gunner most likely did not have a parachute near him. When asked about the place and time of his last contact with Sergeant Haney, he replied:

> In the tail of the plane. Before my jump a sudden maneuver made us lose our balance. When I jumped he was still on the floor of the plane. I think he had the time to jump out after Platoon Leader James Christy, he was the last in the jumping order. ... However, it is possible that, because of the seconds dividing the sudden maneuver and the explosion, he did not manage to regain his balance.[12]

Regarding the remaining crew members it was noted:

> – The last contact with the bombardier, Second Lieutenant Merrill, took place during a routine check of the oxygen system at 1310 h.[13] His further fate remains unknown.
>
> – The bottom turret gunner, Mac Phee, bailed out of the plane. Although whoever provided this information did not speak to him, he does, however, know that Mac Phee was following him toward the tail hatch.[14] The report claimed: "It is possible that because of the intensive fire coming from the German troops on the ground, he was killed while descending on his parachute."[15]
>
> – Regarding Lieutenant Akins and Second Lieutenant Shaw, the testimonies state that both were seen separately in the radio operator's space an hour before the plane was shot down. The last conversation conducted by the co-pilot, Shaw, was heard during the German fighter attack. He was communicating with someone outside of the aircraft.

The report notes that the pilot and co-pilot might not have had the time to bail out. The maneuvers prior to the explosion would seem to indicate that the pilots were still manning the controls.

Our knowledge about the pilots can be supplemented by Mark J. Conversino's *Fighting with the Soviets*. The author cites the testimony of the navigator of the 390th Bomber Group's C Division (serial no. of aircraft: 44-8325), 23-year-old Thomas Stotler. He claims that Akins died as a result of being hit in the face by a shell fired by a German fighter. At the time of his death, the pilot's muscles contracted so violently that the second pilot could not tear his clenched fingers from the yoke. Stotler also stated that he heard on radio channel C the panicked cry of the co-pilot: "The damned cockpit is full of blood!"[16]

As far as the other crew members who had not been mentioned, Flight Officer Berenson and Sergeant Shimshock, the surviving airmen testified that they had no information.

Another eyewitness, then 14-year-old Elżbieta Królak, who lived in an area directly adjacent to Dziekanów Niemiecki, stated that on the day in question a large number of planes flying high above the area between the road and the forest captured her attention. The Germans fired at the planes with everything at their disposal. At the time, the witness's house was the headquarters of a German general and his adjutants, so the shots were also fired from her own backyard. Królak recalls: "I heard a horrific bang. A large pillar of black smoke rose up from the site where the plane crashed. The Germans were very happy as a result of their successful kill, and they raised their arms [in triumph], laughed, and clapped."[17]

Another group of witnesses discovered by the author consisted of three people who were outside of Dziekanów Niemiecki when the plane was shot down. When the American expedition appeared in the area, the then 26-year-old Stanisław Pasternak was in the vicinity of his house in Dziekanów Polski.[18] He recalled that the planes, which moved along the line of the Vistula, were fired on by artillery deployed in the meadows by the road to the wooden bridge being constructed on the river at the time. The sight of the air armada piqued the curiosity of the locals who ventured outside of their homes in an effort to see more, but the German soldiers billeted in the village turned them back. Even so, Pasternak managed to see a bomber shot down above the meadows near the Vistula that disintegrated in the air as its wing became detached from the fuselage and plummeted separately. He also observed how the containers fell out of the wreck on parachutes and fell in the meadows next to Kiełpin. He did not see any other planes dropping containers.

Stefan Szcześniak, then a 16-year-old, happened to be in the village of Kiełpin, which was located about a kilometer away in the direction of Łomianki.[19] According to him, the planes were flying between the Warsaw–Gdańsk road and the forest at an altitude of 800–1,000 m. The Germans shot in their direction using all their weaponry. At that time, he noticed that the bomber was struck in the right wing, which caused the engine to catch fire. Shortly thereafter, the wing fell off and the fuselage began to plummet in a spiral fashion. Meanwhile, the sky filled up with containers attached to parachutes, which the wind dragged in the direction of Kiełpin. There was also a deluge of foil strips which made a distinctive buzzing sound when falling.

An examination of German documents gathered in the Luftwaffenpersonalamt Abschußanerkenntnisse Flak collection from the Bundesarchiv–Militärarchiv Freiburg also shed light on the fate of Lieutenant Akins' bomber "I'll Be Seeing You."[20] These testimonies were gathered initially to determine who was to receive credit for "kills" and to ascertain the number of planes shot down. German records show that there were four anti-aircraft squadrons in the vicinity that could have contributed to the air defense of Warsaw.

The main Axis combat forces in the area included the 27th Panzer Regiment and 1st Hungarian Cavalry Division, as well as detachments of the 4th SS Panzer Corps, and various units and services, such as customs and border guards (its outpost was located in Łomna, on the frontier between the German Reich and the General Government), and units which were only indirectly or not at all mentioned in this collection (but mentioned in other sources), such as elements of the 5th SS Panzer Division "Wiking."

The German documents indicate that the American aircraft arrived from the northwest and cut across the Narew River. They entered the Warsaw area flying in a wide corridor between the villages of Stary Modlin, Stanisławowo, Pomiechowo, and Czarnowo. According to notes taken by the leaders of the Flak batteries, individual American air units appeared in the area between Modlin and Łomianki between 1330 and 1349 h.

A smaller number of these planes, which the Germans estimated at between 20 and 30 machines, moved along the left side of the Vistula. At probably the same time, a second group followed the flow of the river on its eastern bank, only to pass to the western side in the vicinity of Rajszew and Kępa Kiełpińska. The Germans reported this group as a much larger one, numbering about 120 aircraft.

This formation consisted also of the planes of the 390th Bomber Group, or at least some of the bomber wings forming it, including

Bomber Wing B, which included Lieutenant Akins' plane. They moved from the area to the east of the Modlin Fortress above Nowy Dwór toward Rajszew following the clearly visible Warsaw, Jabłonna, and Nowy Dwór road or the Vistula itself. After reaching the area of Rajszew, as mentioned previously, the bombers crossed the Vistula to continue their journey along its other bank toward the objectives.

It is likely that the discrepancies between the various testimonies, including both German and Polish ones, as to the main path of the air expedition and its numerical strength, stem from the fact that individual witnesses saw only its various elements, such as the 95th or 100th Bomber Group.

According to calculations made by German anti-aircraft batteries, the American bombers were flying at various altitudes at speeds of 324, 342, or 360 k/h. In the case of the group sighted above Modlin, the altitude was 4,200 m. In other cases it varied between 4,700, 4,800, and 5,000 m.

Although some German unit reports are missing, the Germans had an estimated fifty-four 88-mm guns in the Modlin and Łomianki area on September 18, 1944. The 50th Motorized Anti-Aircraft squadron reported that its three batteries together fired off a total of 120 projectiles during a period of 11–15 min. Based on the assumption that this generates an average number of 40 shells per battery, all 12 batteries must have fired off about 480 rounds. Since some batteries fired a greater-than-average number of rounds, this is a conservative estimate.

The testimonies of the German soldiers deployed in the area of Dziekanów Polski, Kępa Kiełpińska, and Dziekanów Niemiecki agree that the damaged airplane, Lieutenant Akins' "I'll Be Seeing You," was heading toward the forest after crossing the Vistula. Testimonies given by observers from outside of this area diverged on this point, most likely due to their distance from the place where the aircraft went down. In the fog of war some Germans believed that three aircraft were shot down that day—one or two near Jabłonna and one in Dziekanów Niemiecki—and perhaps yet another one, which supposedly crashed in the area of Kampinos Forest. This opinion was repeated by several witnesses and supported by the commander of 6th Luftflotte, Col. Gen. Robert Ritter von Greim.

According to German witnesses the bomber would have continued its journey toward the area of Wiersze had it not exploded near Dziekanów Niemiecki. A report written by Lt. Karl Lehmann, commander of the 4th Battery, 296th Squadron, which was stationed in the area of Wawrzyszew, indicated that 24-year-old Ensign Paul Lippold of Bamberg, Bavaria, was ordered to locate the crash site. It was believed that the machine crashed in an area 15 km to the northwest of Ożarów in the Kampinos Forest. Lippold could not carry out his mission because he was warned that the forest was in the hands of "bandits."

German reports state that Lieutenant Akins' plane was damaged in the area of Rajszew, but it is impossible to be certain of this. As some documents state, the bomber could have been shot down much earlier. This suggests the participation in this "kill" of batteries as far away as Modlin or those along the plane's path, of the 661st and 22nd Squadrons. While taking this into account we also cannot rule out that the aircraft was damaged even earlier during the German fighter attack.

The credit for shooting down the bomber is often given to Lieutenant Josten, a pilot of Jagdeschwader 51.[21] It is, however, important to point out that these testimonies may be biased and driven by a desire to inflate one's achievements. Furthermore, the testimonies of soldiers manning the anti-aircraft guns and other witnesses claim either that the German fighters were absent from the skies or arrived much later. Only two testimonies mention this. Platoon Leader Aukthun, originally from Poznań, who was deployed in Kazuń Niemiecki at the time, stated: "Only later the enemy was attacked by a few fighters."[22] The second of these two testimonies was provided by secretary Matthae, a customs officer from the post in Łomna: "At the time when the enemy planes were shot down our fighters were not present. They arrived later."[23]

Efforts to determine when Lieutenant Akins' aircraft was damaged are further complicated by the fact that other bombers were being hit by German anti-aircraft fire and fighters as well. This is most likely the reason behind reports claiming that a greater number of planes were shot down.

The reports of the German batteries that were the first to fire at the bombers corroborate each other. Their leaders state that the planes they observed were grouped in four regiments consisting of about 12–30 "Flying Fortresses" each. The first of these regiments was fired upon, but to no avail. The other three regiments were not so lucky, for each lost a plane, which abandoned their formations and began to fall to the ground. These reports mention only a bomber belonging to the fourth regiment in any greater detail. They state that the Germans noted that its right external engine stopped and various parts of the aircraft became detached. As more fire was directed at the bomber, a cloud of black smoke appeared, after which the B-17 was engulfed by flames. The damaged aircraft changed its direction and flew along the road to Warsaw. As it descended the plane clearly lost speed and remained behind as its group continued on its course. Soon thereafter, the burning and disintegrating machine crashed about 15 km from the positions held by the battery.

Based on available eyewitness testimonies, Lieutenant Akins' bomber was hit by a Flak projectile (or projectiles) around 1339 h German time. Of course, the individual testimonies sometimes differ as to the precise time of the "kill," but the time listed above is most often listed by the witnesses. Clearly, right after receiving the first hit, or perhaps another hit which sealed the fate of the plane, the pilot attempted to reach the "emergency area" designated by the American high command, i.e., the Kampinos Forest.[24] For this reason, the damaged bomber abandoned its formation and suddenly changed course. At the same time, "I'll Be Seeing You," and perhaps other aircraft, began to drop their payload soon after crossing the river.

An unnamed German lieutenant, the commander of the 1st Battery of the 296th Squadron, states in his report that the Flak fire dispersed the planes which had been hitherto flying in a tight formation. He also recalls the moment of the "kill" itself:

> In the second group we spotted a flame on the right external engine of the plane. This hit occurred at 1339 h. A streak of white smoke appeared on the plane. The hit machine continued to fly for a short time while constantly descending and then came down in a southwestern direction.... After ditching a large quantity of supply bombs [sic] the group flew in the direction of 5 [5 o'clock?].[25]

It was probably at the same time that the crew began to bail out of the burning aircraft. Given our knowledge of the fate of this crew, it is clear that not all members were able to save themselves. This should not come as a surprise, however, for the time of the flight between the site of the hit (as determined by points on maps attached to the documents) and the crash site (1345 h) was only 6 min. According to Shook's memoir, the plane turned over violently at this time (most likely because the stabilizer fell off), which prevented the crew members gathered by the exit from bailing out of the machine smoothly.

To illustrate these events it is worthwhile to cite available eyewitness testimonies. This includes both individuals who were in the direct vicinity of the events and those further away. The first group included the artillerymen of the 50th Motorized Squadron, who were defending the German river crossing linking both banks of the Vistula at the height of Kępa Kiełpińska. Written on September 18, a combat report of Captain Hartmann, the head of the squadron's second battery, states that the "group" flying above the area defended by their guns "consisted of about 120 Fortress II's, which approached in three waves, each formed into a wedge-like squadron, [and the group was] defended by individual Mustang fighters along its side."[26] Another combat report, prepared by the first battery deployed on the other bank of the Vistula, states that the unit located its target at 1330 h. Two minutes later, the battery opened fire until 1343 h. As noted, a flame appeared on the machine at 1339 h as a result of the barrage.

Captain Hartmann also wrote that the aircraft his unit fired on turned to the right. In the case of the stricken bomber:

> … at about 1339 h a light-colored flame appeared in the right internal engine, which evolved into a long streak of smoke as the plane continued to fly. For a short time, the battered machine accompanied its group, but lost speed and altitude afterward, and fell out of formation to, at first, glide down and, later, to fall in an almost vertical manner.[27]

In its "kill" report, Hartmann's battery also states that soon the damaged plane's right wing fell off and other parts broke off as well. The bomber crashed at 1345 h at a distance of 200 m north of Dziekanów Niemiecki. This information is corroborated by the testimony of the leader of the 1st Battery of the 296th Squadron.

The commander of the 50th Motorized Flak Regiment was also an eyewitness. What particularly captured his attention, he wrote, was the appearance of parachutes. Expecting that an airborne assault had begun, he initiated immediate preparations to repulse it. Because of this, he noticed only the burning machine as it fell out of formation, as well as its disintegration in the air and the crashing of the fragments onto the ground. The commander also pointed out that witness statements and an investigation proved that it was the batteries under his command that were responsible for downing the bomber that crashed in Dziekanów Niemiecki. He firmly rejected any speculations that the machine might have been shot down by other units and ascribes any such impressions to the fact that the Germans employed ammunition with delayed-ignition fuses. He emphasized that there can be no doubt whatsoever that the "kill" could only have been the result of the barrage of his batteries defending the bridge in Kiełpin.

Three days afterwards, while following up on the report, the commander requested that the credit for the "kill" be assigned to a particular battery. He stated that the shot-down aircraft:

> [F]ell vertically with a streak of black smoke. The location of the hit had been visible for quite some time due to a rising mushroom of black smoke. [It was] clearly visible, but it could not be located in the Kampinos Forest because these woods were a strong outpost of the [Polish] bands. The remaining heavy batteries situated on the 40-ton bridge were combating other regiments at this time. Please recognize that the plane was shot down by 1/50.[28]

The testimonies presented above are supplemented by a note made on the same day by a Hungarian NCO named Szarvasy, of the 1st Hungarian Cavalry Division, who was north of Łomianki:

> On September 18, 1944, between 1330 and 1400 h, I saw about sixty four-engine enemy bombers flying toward us in the direction of the 40-ton bridge on the Vistula. We saw clearly that the strong anti-aircraft fire of the 8.8 cm [guns] came from the same direction and [that] one machine was hit. This machine immediately began to burn and fell apart in the air before falling to the ground. Its parts fell to the ground about 1 km away from our position in Łomianki.[29]

Platoon Leader Göttges (a native of Poznań), who served in the 50th Motorized Flak Regiment in the Rajszew area on the other side of the Vistula, was another eyewitness. When recalling the bridge in his testimony, he speaks of a temporary river crossing in the area of Kępa Kiełpińska. This was the bridge that was defended by three Flak batteries deployed on both sides of the river comprising his unit.

> On September 18, 1944 around 1345 h I saw the following from my position on the eastern bank of the 40-ton bridge on the Vistula: One plane became detached from the second regiment of four-engine enemy bombers which were flying in from the north and had been fired upon by heavy Flak batteries in Modlin. Its right wing was already burning when the plane flew nearby my location. An "e" rose (from a northern direction) to a height of 3,200 m when the wing began to burn. Later, it appears, the plane first attempted to conduct an emergency landing, [but] this failed, and he crashed to the ground in the direction of Warsaw and caught on fire as a result of the impact. I cannot provide the exact distance because we were on airborne assault alert. Furthermore, the area where the access road to the bridge intersected the road to Warsaw was the crash site for the fragments of an aircraft from the last regiment which had earlier been consumed by flames and disintegrated in the air.[30]

Platoon Leader Göttges also wrote that, like others, he witnessed the shooting-down of two additional aircraft which, as he states, "rumbled down to the ground in a southeastern direction from my position."[31] He emphasizes, however, that his platoon did not shoot down these planes. They were out of range due to the altitude at which the bombers were flying and the weaponry they were equipped with—20 mm cannons.[32]

In the days following the events of September 18, 1944, all of the individual German units lobbied to receive credit for the "kills" scored that day. The requests reveal a spirit of rivalry, both between the various units and the individual batteries. The extant documents include the request of the commander of the 77th Motorized Flak Regiment, who asked that the "kills" be credited to the 1st and 2nd Batteries, 661st Squadron, as well as 1st and 3rd Batteries, 22nd Squadron. On 1 October 1944, less than 2 weeks later, the commander of the 6th Luftflotte, Col. Gen. Ritter von Greim, followed his lead:

> The shooting-down of an enemy Fortress II-type aircraft, which occurred on September 18, 1944 at 1347 h in the area of the village [Dziekanów] Niemiecki by the 1. – 4./gem. Flakabt. 661 (v) with the collaboration of the 1. and 3./

Flakregt. 22 was proven beyond any doubts by the witnesses located on the ground. This refers to 1 of the 3 aircraft shot down on 18 September 1944.

I am requesting that this be recognized.[33]

Thus, based on an assessment of the witness testimonies, supported by the opinion of Colonel General Greim, the destruction of, or cooperation in, the shooting down (in various configurations) of this and two other bombers (which the Germans were certain to have shot down), was also attributed to two other units of the anti-aircraft defense, the 50th Motorized Battery and 1st Battery, 296th Squadron, by a decision of the Oberkommando der Luftwaffe made in October and November 1944.

CHAPTER 6

Lost Over Warsaw

When "I'll Be Seeing You" was hit, the crew attempted to bail out, but due to the damage suffered by the aircraft and fatal wounds suffered by some of the crew, not all made it out of the burning plane. But crew members who made it out of a dying craft were not out of danger. Parachutes could be damaged even before being deployed or malfunction on their own. As eyewitness reports on the ground show, German forces in the area were firing into the air with every weapon available. Shrapnel from exploding rounds, live rounds, and pieces of the damaged aircraft presented extreme danger to crew in their parachutes. Descending crew could be hit and killed or their vulnerable parachutes could also be hit, causing them to crash to the ground.

Nothing better illustrates the dangers facing the surviving crew of "I'll Be Seeing You" than the account of Marcus Shook. He recalled:

> I was falling quietly until I heard some kind of shooting right above the ground. When I felt a stinging pain in my left thigh I realized that these were shots fired from revolvers and rifles. I pulled up my legs and tucked my knees under my chin to become the smallest possible target. Shortly after I released my legs once again, I was shot again and the bullet caused a complicated fracture right above the right ankle. This was my second wound.

> Once I landed on a freshly mowed field, I was easily apprehended before I managed to free myself from the parachute. Luckily, the weather was peaceful and the wind did not pull me along the ground. An officer in a black uniform, who commanded the unit which captured me, demanded my "pistole." My answer of "Nein pistole" exhausted my German vocabulary. He was surprised that I didn't have any weapons. I think "Snuffy" [Merrill] was the only crew member during

the flight who had a gun. At the moment I was captured the time was about 1300 h or maybe a bit later, so it is debatable whether at the moment when Christy and I jumped we were at a higher altitude than 3,000 ft.[1] From the location at which I was captured I was taken to an interrogation to a field command post in some old house, where, as I recall, I only gave my last name, rank, and number.[2]

In his account written at end of the war, Shook also wrote that, while descending on his parachute, he gazed down and noticed two parachutes far to his rear. He further added that, after being captured by the soldiers of the German armored division, he received immediate first aid. He was then taken to the field command post, where the soldiers and officers who interrogated the American airman treated him decently and adequately to his rank and the wounds he suffered.

Soon after the American planes passed by, the Germans stationed in Dziekanów Polski ordered the locals to assemble. According to Stanisław Pasternak, soon after the expedition disappeared a man resettled from Pomerania was ordered by the Germans to go from house to house informing all those who lived near the chapel located by the commons that they are to assemble before a home housing a German medical post.[3] Simultaneously, the Germans were also herding people from the road running through the village to the meadow.

The crowd, which had been assembled in a hurry, was threatened with execution given their implied connection to the partisans for whom the drops had been intended. Here they stood packed on a small meadow and were questioned about the American airmen. The villagers were also threatened with death for sheltering the Allied pilots or refusing to turn them in.

While standing in the crowd, Pasternak suddenly noticed an American airman with a leg wound who was brought by the Germans by car.[4] Having been deprived of his shoes, he stood only in his socks in the gate of a neighboring property where a German soldier was billeted.[5] Soon after his appearance the villagers were sent back home and the airman was taken somewhere in a military vehicle.

Polish eyewitness Klemens Bogurat recalled:

The plane fell not far from the Warsaw–Kazuń road, near a big linden tree. Its shot-off tail landed some 800 m further, in the area of today's elementary school in

P-51C Mustang, piloted by Lt. Joseph J. Vigna, 358th Fighter Squadron, 355th Fighter Group, 8th Air Force. (Drawing by Robert Gretzyngier)

De Havilland D.H. 89 Mosquito, 653rd Light Bomber Squadron, 25th Bomb Group, 8th Air Force. (Drawing by Robert Gretzyngier)

B-17G Flying Fortress, "I'll Be Seeing You," 568th Bomber Squadron, 390th Bomb Group, 8th Air Force. (Drawing by Robert Gretzyngier)

P-51D Mustang, piloted by Lt. Robert O. Peters, 358th Fighter Squadron, 355th Fighter Group, 8th Air Force. (Drawing by Robert Gretzyngier)

15 September 1944: The operations room of the 355th Fighter Group showing the proposed route of the *Frantic* 7 mission. (Photo by Bill Marshall)

Crew of the B-17G "Bugs Bunny," 568th Squadron, 390th Bomb Group. Front row, left to right: Lt. Paul Hibbard (pilot), Lt. James R. O'Neil (co-pilot), Lt. Jack P. Stovall (navigator), A. J. Rubenstein (bombardier, not present for the *Frantic* 7 mission). Top row, left to right: Pfc. Raymond Foppiano (top turret gunner), Lester H. Baumgarte (radio operator), Sgt. Jack G. Edwards (waist gunner), Pvt. William Fletcher (waist gunner), George R. Waite (ball turret gunner), Sgt. Robert Underwood (tail gunner). (Photo: 390th Bomb Group Memorial Museum)

Crew of the B-17 "I'll Be Seeing You," during training at Drew Field, Tampa, Florida, 1944. Front row from left: Walter Shimshock (Szymczak) (rear gunner), Daniel Weinberg (ball turret gunner), Paul F. Haney (waist gunner), Frank P. De Cillis (top turret gunner, engineer). Back row from left: Marcus Shook (radio operator), Francis E. Akins (pilot), Forrest Shaw (co-pilot), Myron S. Merrill (bombardier). (Photo: the late Garnett L. Akins Rainey)

Lt. Robert O. Peters, 358th Squadron, 355th Fighter Group. (Photo: 355th Fighter Group Association)

Lt. Joseph J. Vigna, 358th Squadron, 355th Fighter Group. (Photo: 355th Fighter Group Association)

Navigator Ely Berenson (left) with co-pilot 2nd Lt. Forrest D. Shaw. (Photo: the late Garnett L. Akins Rainey)

Co-pilot 2nd Lt. Forrest D. Shaw (left) with pilot Lt. Francis E. Akins. (Photo: the late Garnett L. Akins Rainey)

Sgt. Vincent J. Stefanek, at the waist gunner position. (Photo: Vincent J. Stefanek)

18 September 1944: P-51 Mustangs of the 355th Fighter Group warming up their engines prior to the start of Operation *Frantic* 7. (Photo by Bill Marshall)

P-51C Mustang, flown by Lt. Joseph J. Vigna, shot down 18 September 1944. (Photo: Ken Wells)

On the way to Warsaw: A B-17G piloted by Lt. Albert G. Grigg, "My Blue Heaven" of the 100th Bomb Group. (Photo by Bill Marshall)

Crew positions on "I'll Be Seeing You":
1. Pilot and commanding officer, Lt. Francis E. Akins
2. Co-pilot, 2nd Lt. Forrest D. Shaw
3. Navigator Ely Berenson
4. Bombardier 2nd Lt. Myron S. Merrill
5. Top turret gunner, M. Sgt. Frank P. De Cillis
6. S. Sgt. George Mac Phee (Ball Turret Gunner)
7. S. Sgt. Paul Haney (Waist Gunner)
8. T. Sgt. Marcus Shook (Radio Operator)
9. S. Sgt. Walter Shimshock (Tail Gunner)
10. Sgt. James Christy (Waist Gunner)

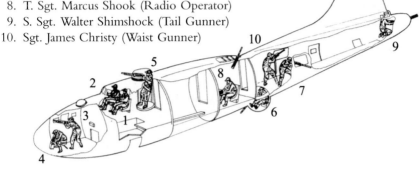

Lt. Francis E. Akins and his wife Garnett L. Akins. (Photo: the late Garnett L. Akins Rainey)

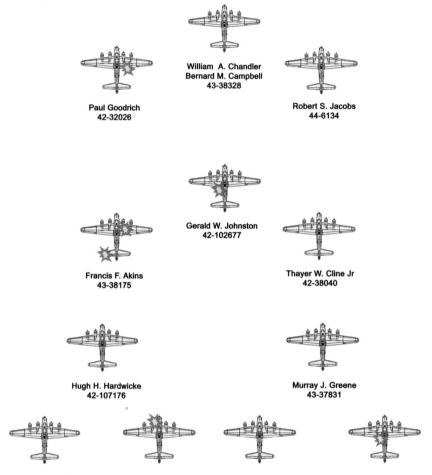

Formation of B-17 on the approach to Warsaw, showing location of "I'll Be Seeing You" piloted by Francis Akins. (Illustration by Jerzy Szczesniak)

Dziekanów Leśny.[6] I did not see any aircraft explosions. I know from the latter-day tales told by locals that one airman was captured on the other side of the Vistula, in the locality of Rajszew. I saw another airman, a clean-cut, swarthy, and handsome young man, standing in the entrance gate leading to the current-day property no. 309 [in Dziekanów Polski]. He was wearing a light, khaki-colored uniform with no headgear. We looked at each other. He did not appear to be wounded.

I returned to the site of the wreckage 2 days later, even though the penalty for this was death, and I gazed at the equipment. I saw machine guns and ammunition belts. The plane was facing in the direction of Warsaw and its entire rear end had been torn off right behind the wings.

I heard from the local people that the bodies of the dead airmen were found a few meters away from the wreckage, as they had been tossed out of the plane at the moment of impact.

Soon thereafter the wreck was taken by the Germans. The boxes, which contained mainly weapons, revolvers and Sten machine guns, were emptied and abandoned by the Germans, only to the later utilized by the locals on their farms.

Eyewitness Skarbek-Kruszewski's testimony also confirms the statement of Klemens Bogurat. He stated that the Germans hauled away the remains of the bomber. Skarbek-Kruszewki noted that:

A few days after we spotted a large number of American planes, our truck brought in parts of two American Flying Fortresses that had been shot down. During break at work everyone came to look at the large wings, crushed fuselage and engines. Their size made an impression on us all. The wheel stood as high as a man. These were four-engine models of the B-17 types. A large group congregated around one engine.

A distraught young man yelled out: "Look! He was killed here. You can see blood and his body." Coming closer, I could spot shredded pieces of human flesh within the crushed fuselage, and I could also see a boot with a piece of the dead pilot's leg in the cockpit. This was all that was left of the pilot, who was destroyed along with his machine. ... People began to tear metal pipes and wires from the blood-drenched fuselage. "Look what a great part! It will be perfect for making moonshine!" someone proudly displayed his treasure.

Another man, in turn, attempted to obtain rubber, which could be useful for repairing shoes, from the fuel tank, while in the author's presence. The witness concluded his testimony by adding that the plane was completely looted within several days.

According to Ryszard Szczesniak, the damaged aircraft crashed in the fields between the Warsaw–Modlin road and the buildings of Dziekanów Niemiecki. According to the same testimony, the plane did not explode at the moment of impact. Its nose pointed in the direction of Warsaw. The wreckage, when observed from afar, appeared to be whole.

The witness was part of this crowd and noticed that an airman the Germans were escorting from the direction of Kiełpin appeared on the road. He was tall, young, bare-headed, lightly dressed, and clearly limping. This was probably Marcus Shook. The escorting Germans brought him into the house. After receiving assurance that none of the villagers had seen the remaining airmen, the gathered villagers were sent home.

After his capture and interrogation, Shook was sent to the field hospital, where his wounds were dressed and his broken leg was reset and placed in a cast. One German bullet from the ground passed through his left thigh, while the second one caused a complicated fracture of his right ankle.

During the next several days (September 20–23), the airman was interned in a camp along with Polish prisoners, most likely captured Warsaw insurgents. Afterward, he was transported to a field hospital in Łódź in an ambulance from an unspecified location. After spending the night at the hospital, Shook was moved by train to Wolsztyn. He was admitted into the Reserve Lazarett Wollstein hospital on the premises of the POW camp located there on September 24, 1944.[7] The Red Cross post in Geneva was informed of his arrival two days later by a letter sent by a clandestine source working in the hospital. We may assume that as a result of this letter Shook was contacted by a representative of the Red Cross on October 22. Consequently, information of his fate was passed on to the U.S. legation in Bern, Switzerland.

According to Shook's testimony, the Wolsztyn camp housed a large number of Soviet POWs, a few British ones, and a few captives of other nationalities, including two Americans. The hospitalized patients were cared for by British medical personnel, and, later, Poles taken prisoner during the September campaign of 1939. Shook remembered several names: orderly Stanisław Marecki, doctors Capt. Zygmunt Dziembowski and Lt. Bogumił Gontarski, and orderly Stefan Kulczak, who performed an unspecified function.[8] Shook spoke highly of his caretakers, recalling their excellent work in difficult conditions, which was a source of inspiration for the prisoners during these hard times.

Shook's testimony is enhanced by one of the two above-mentioned Americans, 2nd Lt. Francis R. Clark. He had been shot down during a bombing raid on Blechhammer near Tuchów on October 13, 1944.[9] Clark belonged to the 465th Bomber Group, and was brought to the hospital in Wolsztyn along with one of his crew members, Sergeant Edward J. Chapin.[10] In his memoirs Clark writes that, after reaching the camp, they were housed in barracks, along with four other soldiers, including: fellow American Shook; two Frenchmen, Lieutenant Cutay and Sergeant Delalande; and a Norwegian officer, Lieutenant Holter.

Clark recalls that Shook initially treated the newcomers with distrust and did not speak to them, suspecting that they might collaborate with the Germans in an effort to obtain information from him. Later, he admitted to his disguised joy on hearing his mother tongue after a long hiatus. (Dr. Dziembowski was the only other person who could speak English in the camp.) In one of the later conversations, he also revealed that he was shot down during an airdrop for Warsaw, and was fired on by automatic weapons, suffering a leg fracture while in his parachute.

Soon thereafter, the three Americans in the camp were joined by five U.S. officers from Oflag 64 Altburgund–Szubin and an accompanying physician, Lieutenant Godgrey.[11]

Clark recalled that the conditions in which he was hospitalized at the camp infirmary were good. The barracks were clean and warm. The prisoners were never hungry and received a regular weekly package from the American Red Cross. Additionally, contrary to the official ban, they traded cigarettes and chocolate with the German guards in exchange for fresh bread, potatoes, and vegetables. At one time, they also wrote a request to the older camp, Oflag 64, as a result of which they later received a few basic items indispensable to them as POWs.

Given that both Shook and Clark were bedridden, while others, such as Sergeant Chapin, were not completely independent, they were assisted in their daily activities by the Polish orderly Stanisław Marecki, as well as the other Poles, doctors Dziembowski and Gontarski, and orderly Kulczak.

On January 15, 1945, the Prisoner of War Information Service/ Bureau first sent Shook's mother a letter with concrete information of her son's fate. He had been considered MIA prior to this. The letter briefly described the circumstances in which Shook was wounded and provided information on his successful convalescence and attempts (as of October 24, 1944) to stand up and ambulate independently using crutches.

On January 21, the prisoners immediately noticed signs of chaos around the camp. They could also hear the sounds of battle approaching ever closer. During the next few days, part of the German camp crew suddenly disappeared, while the camp commandant's offices became the site of the frantic burning of documents. In the next several days, these omens brought a change in the prisoners' fate.

At around 0200 h on January 26 the Red Army entered the camp. Soon, the celebrating with the "liberators" began. The Soviets were quite curious about the Americans and eagerly peeked into the barracks. They were friendly, but the mutual relations were not without incident, such as when a drunken Red Army soldier put a gun up to Shook's head and stole his watch. Clark recalls that the ex-POWs did not initially leave the premises of the camp, fearing that they would be mistaken for Germans and accidentally shot by the Soviets in their ruthless hunt for any remaining German troops hiding out in the area of Wolsztyn.

Already on the next day apprehension set in regarding the future fate of the ex-POWs. The men even elected a delegation, which reached the Soviet commandant of Wolsztyn, but returned empty-handed.

Because the hitherto regularly arriving Red Cross packages had now ceased, and the food offered by the Soviets was scarce, hunger soon set in among the former captives. After the initial period of disorganization, the Soviets also began to guard the camp. Leaving the camp required the permission of the commandant, but Clark would sometimes sneak out in search of food through a hole in the fence. On February 20, Clark, Chapin, and another American used the same gap to secretly escape from the camp. Traveling by foot or via various random modes of transportation, they headed eastward and finally reached the port of Odessa on March 5, 1945.[12] A few days later they were allowed to board a British ship and reached Italy.

Shook's fate was somewhat different. Because of problems in organizing the necessary means of transportation, he left the Wolsztyn camp, along with a group of American, British, and French ex-POWs, only in March 1945.[13] They traveled first by bus, and then on board multiple cargo trains (with numerous stops), until finally reaching Odessa. During this journey, Shook also found himself in Warsaw, which had been the objective of his crew's ill-fated flight of September 18, 1944. The sheer scope of the devastation he saw in Warsaw was etched in his memory forever.

After boarding the British ship in Odessa, the group was taken to Naples in Italy. From there they traveled by airplane to Casablanca in Morocco. Shook eventually made his way to the United States in May 1945. From New York City he was transported to Camp Shelby, an Army training camp in Mississippi. Until his return to the States, Shook knew nothing of the fate of his fellow crew members. Following a 45-day leave, he returned to the ranks of the military at Homestead in Florida and was eventually demobilized in October 1945. Shook was awarded the Purple Heart, the Air Medal, and the Prisoner of War Medal.

It is difficult to unequivocally ascertain what happened to the remaining airmen on September 18. The men must have remembered little, given the intensity and violent nature of their experiences, a growing anxiety for their own fates, and the roar of the engines and the noise of the Flak fire, which compounded the confusion.

The time that has elapsed since the events described here meant that, at the time this book was written, only two individuals who witnessed the shooting-down of Lieutenant Akins' plane and, simultaneously, happened to be in or near Dziekanów Niemiecki at the time, were still alive. Their testimonies, however valuable, do not provide answers to all the questions. Fortunately, two testimonies written down many years before survived.

In 1981 a resident of Dziekanów Niemiecki, Janina Niegodzisz, stated that she saw one crew member descending on a parachute in the area of the village. According to this testimony, the young man was waving a handkerchief, thereby signaling a willingness to surrender, but was shot by an approaching German soldier in a black panzer unit uniform.[14] The brief description of the events is elaborated on in a postwar statement, although the circumstances in which it was prepared remain unclear:

> Statement of September 28, 1945 on a German crime. On the day of September 19, 1944, an American plane was shot down above Dziekanów Leśny in [the parish of] Cząstków in Warsaw County. The airmen dropped into the area of the aforementioned locality, some on parachutes, and some in the airplane. [One] airman flying on a parachute was shot down with a revolver right above the ground, in spite of showing the Germans with a handkerchief that he was surrendering. [The Germans] didn't pay attention to the handkerchief waving, however, and killed the above mentioned airman using small arms just above the ground.
>
> From among the plane's entire crew, only one airman fell [to the ground] alive, although he had suffered multiple wounds. The wounded American soldier was taken by the Germans to the command post [for questioning and there is] no information about him.
>
> The Germans stripped all the dead American airmen of their clothing and left the bodies to lie in the fields naked.[15]

On September 18 Józef Sopiński, an eyewitness discovered 60 years later, was working in the field at the edge of the village of Dziekanów Niemiecki. In spite of the passage of decades, he remembered well the panic of the hiding Germans and the crescendo of guns firing at the aircraft which remained behind its formation. He also saw two airmen dressed in leather suits, who descended while signaling with their handkerchief their intention to surrender. A German soldier, who had been hiding in the crown of one of two chestnut trees growing nearby, moved in their direction.[16] Using his submachine gun, he shot one airman in the head, killing him, and sliced another in half by peppering his abdomen with bullets. The German immediately tore the leather suit from the first body. Because the other airman's suit was drenched with blood, the German ordered a group of young Polish refugees from Warsaw to remove the clothing. When they steadfastly refused, he chased them away while cussing "Polnische Schweine!" (Polish pigs). The dead American remained in his suit. Sopiński adds that the bodies of the remaining airmen were buried only in their underclothes.[17]

Elżbieta Królak stated that the plane crashed in the fields belonging to the village's German residents located between Dziekanów Niemiecki and the road running toward Gdańsk. The Germans did not allow anyone to approach the crash site. Only after the situation calmed down, they began to deliver various kinds of packages to her property using vehicles. When asked about the airmen, Królak stated that "he landed somewhere in the fields behind the road watchman's post between Kiełpin and Dziekanów Polski. The airman suffered a leg wound."[18] The witness, who did not personally see the crash or the capture of the airman, found out about his wound from her younger sister, who understood the language and eavesdropped on the conversations of the Nazis quartered in her house. As she continued, Królak also recalled that the Germans brought a parachute to her house, which she associated with the airman.

When asked about the bodies of the airmen, the witness replied: "I also saw the bodies of four airmen, which were brought here by buggy, but the men did not allow us to approach. The airmen were large. We felt really bad for them. We cried."

The dead men were buried in a wide ditch that had been dug in a place also indicated by other witnesses. It was located in the area of the present-day bus stop in Dziekanów Leśny.[19] The bodies were buried in their clothes and were placed next to each other.

Królak recalls that at the time she did not see any containers with parachutes or any other airmen. She did remember that others said that the airplane's wing had landed in a separate location.

Stefan Szcześniak spotted two airmen in the area of the village. According to information gathered from people who viewed the body, one of them dropped onto the ground as a consequence of his parachute being peppered with bullets. His corpse lay in a field about 30 m from the main road running through Łomianki.[20] Another airman, who was lucky enough to survive, landed using his parachute in the area of Kiełpin some 70–80 m behind a local barn.[21] He was quickly apprehended by the Germans who did not use any violence against him. According to Stefan Szcześniak, such German behavior stemmed from the fact that they now realized, upon seeing the containers, that this was only a supply airdrop, and not the airborne assault they initially feared when they spotted the first parachutes.

Two soldiers of the labor battalion stationed in the village brought the captive to a medical post located not far from his landing site.[22] The airman was wearing a green uniform and was walking only in his socks. He also had two leg wounds. Due to the passage of time, the witness is not completely sure, but strongly believes that both were right-leg thigh wounds. Having been escorted to the medical post, the airman did not sit on the bench located in the front yard, but stood leaning against the fence.

Soon, a military ambulance arrived and an officer, who was also a physician, stepped out. He shook the airman's hand and spoke to him for a while in English. He also offered the wounded man a cigarette, but the American refused and took out his own cigarettes from his upper left shirt pocket. A while later, the airman was assisted by two soldiers and climbed into the ambulance, which departed toward Łomianki. Most likely, according to the witness, he was taken to Dąbrowa or Łomianki, where the Germans maintained their military hospitals at the time.

Meanwhile, the Germans were gathering the contents of the dropped containers, which included the revolvers, food, milk, and cigarettes seen by Szcześniak.

A different reconstruction of the events in question, albeit from a different perspective, was provided by another witness: the then 26-year-old Franciszka Kłódkiewicz, then a resident of Kiełpin.[23] As Kłódkiewicz recalls, the Germans were at the time stationed on her family's property. Seeing the airplanes and parachutes, one of the soldiers yelled out: "Airborne assault!" Since the Germans ordered the inhabitants to hide, a nearby cellar served as the shelter. Franciszka Kłódkiewicz recalls:

> When the shooting started, Father yelled out "don't leave the cellar!" But he was curious and peeked out of the door. Father called me and said: "Come and see: some sort of tarp is falling down." They shot as he was falling. I was looking at this boy as he was coming down. When they noticed he was sitting [the man, the German] yelled out not to shoot. "Stop shooting!" he yelled out loudly. They missed him. And one of them yelled out clearly "He fell!" I flew out of the cellar

and I was looking, because I saw that they weren't shooting anymore so I wasn't afraid. Father says: "Come, we will go between the barns."

The parachuting airman landed in a field behind the barn line belonging to the Bączek family.[24] The witness did not see the moment of the airman's landing which was blocked by the barn. When she approached with her father the airman was already on the ground: "When I got there they already had him in their hands. They detached that parachute from him. The soldiers took him but didn't harm him. Later they somehow placed him on the car, drove around the village, and parked on the street." Kłódkiewicz elaborated: "They treated him well, [and] they helped him walk to the street, where he got onto the car and sat on this car."

Propelled by curiosity and encouraged by her father, the witness ran out onto the road running through Kiełpin:

> I was really curious. Father says "Go and look [at what is happening] on the street. They won't hurt you." I hurried over and I saw a truck there. The airman was sitting in his socks on the vehicle. He wasn't wounded at all. The poor boy was sitting there looking very sad. He was a young and nice-looking boy. [He was] tall. The German offered him a cigarette. He didn't want to take the cigarette, but he took the entire package when offered. He took one out and [the German] gave him a light. I was looking at him and said [to myself]: "Such a handsome boy and [he was only wearing] socks. How is he going to walk around now?" Later the truck with the prisoner departed.

According to Kłódkiewicz's testimony, while the bombers forming part of the expedition passed by, a lone plane was flying from the direction of the Vistula moving between Kiełpin Lake and the river. He dropped his cargo behind the lake and flew away toward the forest. The witness knew from the testimonies of others that the plane later crashed in the fields by the forest in the area of Dziekanów Niemiecki and was consumed by flames. The rest of its crew perished there. The charred body of one of the airmen was supposedly transported by a now deceased inhabitant of the village by the name of Dąbrowski.

When everything calmed down, one of the Germans told them to go to the fields to see "the treasure lying there." Once they reached the location, however, everything was gone. The parachutes and containers were taken by the Germans from Kiełpin and Kępa Kiełpińska. Some of the captured loot was also brought to the witness's yard, which became the collection site. She recalled:

> [There was] chocolate, weapons, and food. Oh Jesus, all of those parachutes and everything else. We had two Ukrainian women here who knew how to sew and we also had a tailor. He made dresses for them from the parachutes. The other parachutes were wound up and taken away. They took the food. I have no idea where it all went.

Before sunset on the very same day, Stefan Szcześniak and a Silesian, who had deserted from the German army and was hiding in the village, went to see the shot-down bomber. He remembered that the nose of the wreckage had torn into the ground and the plane was leaning to its side. One of the wings lay about 50–100 m away. The aluminum fuselage had disintegrated, which made it easier to look inside. Within the plane the bodies of three green-clad airmen were strewn throughout, while one airman was still sitting on the left side in the cockpit.[25]

The second of the previously mentioned witnesses appeared in the area of Dziekanów Niemiecki just before the events described by Stefan Szcześniak. During the late noon hours of the same day, Pasternak headed to Dziekanów Niemiecki on a horse-drawn buggy to collect the potatoes that had been prepared before noon. Once there, he was stopped by a German soldier, who ordered him and another unknown man (who was not a resident of the village) to collect the bodies and move them, using the plane doors as a platform, to a prepared grave.

The men thus moved the body of one airman. Later, as the end of the day approached and the task proved difficult, the German allowed them to use Pasternak's buggy. They then collected five to six bodies in the field.

The bodies lay in an arable field near the wreckage between the main road to Modlin and a road running through the village. The wingless fuselage had broken in two, right behind the wing roots. A fragment devoid of the horizontal stabilizers rested near the front part of the fuselage. The wings lay separately. Numerous parts of the machine were strewn all over the field.

Near the front part of the wreck's fuselage there were two or three corpses. Two more men were lying, at a distance from one another, near the rear end. Approximately 300–400 m away, near a tree growing by the road linking Dziekanów Niemiecki with the road to Modlin, rested an engine with a fragment of the wing.[26] There was another dead body next to it. One of the dead airmen had suffered serious head injuries. They were missing their boots and some were also undressed. Some were still wearing their uniforms while others wore only their undershirts and long underwear. Pasternak speculated that the Germans looted whatever items were in decent condition, leaving only those which had been destroyed during the crash. The witness noticed that none of the fallen had their parachutes. He does not remember whether this was so in the case of all the airmen, but some of the fallen were certainly lying in craters which were likely formed as a result of their fall onto the ground.

The men loaded the bodies they found onto the buggy and then transported them to the village. A large ditch had already been dug near the main road and next to the willow trees growing in the vicinity. The corpses were laid out next to it. When the men finished the task they were ordered to perform, the sun was already setting.

Pasternak does not know who dug the grave, nor does he know who buried the dead or when. After transporting the bodies, he was shaken by his experience and returned home in a hurry. He remembered that on the same day news spread that, in addition to the bomber, the Germans had also shot down an American fighter.

In light of the above testimonies there are additional items that are interesting but not easily verifiable:

- An alarm telegram sent by the commander of the Home Army on September 25 via a radio station in the Warsaw area to the staff of the Commander-in-Chief:[27] "On the 18th our plane was shot down and one airman jumped out above Dąbrowa near Warsaw. He had a broken leg and was captured. He suffered a lot while being tested without any medical supplies. He behaved like a soldier. After being tested he was shot. His name was not ascertained. His description: tall and blonde, about 22 years old, had a photograph of young girl with him."[28]
- A fragment of Prime Minister Mikołajczyk's speech intended for occupied Poland and published in *Dziennik Polski i Dziennik Żołnierza* [The Polish Daily and the Soldier's Daily] on September 21, 1944:[29] "The

day of September 18 brings you great assistance from Great Britain which is carried by American airmen, the same airmen who know that their brothers-in-arms who had been shot-down over Poland were rescued from German captivity and liberated by a Home Army unit."[30]

• The testimony of Capt. Adolf Pilch "Dolina," the commander of the Home Army regiment Palmiry-Młociny: "The Germans shot down an American plane near Warsaw, [and] two jumped out and could not be found. One mulatto or black man was brutally beaten to death by the Germans near Dziekanów."[31]

It is difficult to find the origin of Captain Pilch's mention of the dark skin color of one of the airmen. At this time racial segregation was the rule both in American society and the U.S. military. This was one of the reasons why African-Americans served in only two air units: the 332nd Fighter Group and the 477th Bomber Group. The latter was not involved in the action.

Two of the three quotes cited above corroborate the murder of an airman in the area of Dziekanów [Niemiecki], and one also points to an attempt by Home Army partisans to locate the shot-down airmen. Unfortunately, this is not confirmed by any of the testimonies with which the author is familiar or by the few surviving "Kampinos" Group documents stored at the Archiwum Akt Nowych [Archive of New Records] in Warsaw.

According to the testimony of the previously mentioned Janina Niegodzisz, the bodies of the dead airmen were buried with the permission of the Germans by the Polish inhabitants of Dziekanów Niemiecki on a date as late as September 20, 1944. The bodies were accordingly wrapped in bed sheets and buried in a mass grave alongside the main road running through the village. After the conclusion of the war, Janina Niegodzisz's husband, Stanisław, a wartime partisan, installed a gravestone on the spot of the airmen's final resting place. Their grave was surrounded by a small fence and marked by a black marble stone hauled from a nearby cemetery of German colonists.

Just like the earlier fragment of the testimony, the following also supplements the previously mentioned statement from September 28, 1945, which states that:

The population of Dziekanów Leśny collected and buried the bodies of all seven fallen American airmen in a common grave in the village of Dziekanów Leśny.

After the enemy retreated from the area, the local population fenced off the grave of the American soldiers, who died a heroic death on Polish soil, commemorating them with a 5-min period of silence and entrusting its care to the local elementary school in Dziekanów Polski.

The following witnesses, who gathered the bodies of the fallen airmen from the fields into a common grave, testify to the above: Wincenty Pieniek, Marian Zaborowski, Szczepan Mazanko, Janina Niegodzisz, Jan [Stawski].[32]

German reports pertaining to the shooting-down of the enemy plane by the individual Flak batteries also provide the number of captured or killed airmen, in addition to other details. Since this information is always presented in a brief manner, and the personal information of the POWs is never mentioned, it is impossible to utilize this information to reconstruct the further fate of the individual airmen. Unfortunately, this also applies to the testimonies of eyewitnesses, who focused exclusively on the events and their own experiences. Only one eyewitness testimony, written by a German soldier serving in the 27th Panzer Regiment and deployed in Dziekanów Niemiecki at the time, mentions the fate of the anonymous airmen. The testimony includes not only data on the number of men taken prisoner, but also a mention of those killed in action. The German mentioned that one airman died instantly, while another was captured and taken to the headquarters of the 19th Panzer Division. This fact also appears in the previously mentioned eyewitness testimony included in the "Statement of September 28, 1945 on a German Crime."

Captain Becker of the 27th Panzer Regiment stated in a testimony from September 18, 1944:

I was in [Dziekanów] Niemiecki (YJ 1b) and I saw how one burning aircraft from the last regiment of four-engine planes flew in from the north, disintegrated above this locality, and crashed to the ground in pieces. Two crew members jumped out on parachutes, [and] one of them died instantly. The other, having suffered heavy wounds, was delivered to the command post of the 19 Panz. Div.

The seven other dead aircrew members were to be found strewn around the crash site.[33]

In the case of the three testimonies presented below, which deal with the prisoner (or prisoners, when the testimonies mention two individuals), there are only short statements paraphrased by those describing the events in question. All of these testimonies are drawn from reports generated by batteries stationed in the direct neighborhood of Dziekanów Polski and Rajszew. The report written by the German lieutenant commanding the 3rd Battery of the 50th Motorized Flak Regiment introduces an element of confusion into this reasoning. The officer stated that "not one captive was delivered from the shot-down machine."[34]

The report of the 1st Battery of the 50th Motorized Flak Regiment from the shot-down machine stated that the bomber groups' task was "to drop supply bombs [sic] in the Warsaw area for the insurgents. A larger share of these bombs fell in the outlying area of the 1st Battery of the 50th Motorized Flak Regiment, however."[35]

Another report from September 18, 1944, by the 1st Battery of the 296th Squadron, stated that "the group dropped a large quantity of supply bombs with parachutes destined for parts of Warsaw occupied by the bandits, but they failed to reach them, and all of them fell in areas held by our troops instead. According to the testimony of the captured crew member, the planes took off from England before noon on September 18."[36]

A third German report stated that:

> … the group dropped a large quantity of supplies on parachutes. The supplies were intended for the insurgents in Warsaw, but fell almost exclusively outside of the city itself onto our positions and failed to reach the destination. According to a statement by a captured crew member from the shot-down machine, the unit took off from England; the group departed to the east.[37]

The German testimonies presented above list not only information about the captives but also perpetuate information appearing earlier of a large supply airdrop in the area where the 50th Regiment was stationed.[38] This airdrop, clearly larger than one conducted by only one machine (12 containers on average), is also mentioned by another witness, Dziekanów Polski resident Ryszard Szcześniak. When speaking of the events of September 18, Szcześniak recalls that the Germans offered him some of the condensed milk captured from the airdrop in his own yard. Since some of the Germans could also communicate in Polish, Szcześniak remembers them mentioning that the milk came from containers which fell in the area between Dziekanów and Kiełpin.

As in the case with the POWs, data permitting us to ascertain the exact unit to which the shot-down bomber belonged is mentioned by reports generated by only two batteries located closest to the crash site and belonging to the 50th Squadron. These were positioned in the Dziekanów Polski–Kępa Kiełpińska area. These reports mention the tactical number and insignia of the 390th Bomber Group, the letter "J." The inclusion of such details suggests that the soldiers manning these batteries could have been the only ones to have been at the crash site and who could have inspected the wreckage. Interestingly, and contrary to the role in locating the aircraft ascribed to the above battery, is the fact that only one report, written on September 18 by two batteries from the 661st Squadron from the relatively distant area of Modlin, provides the accurate number of airmen who were killed and survived: eight and two. All other reports that touch on these statistics speak of seven dead and two captured airmen, which differs from the numerical strength of the crew of "I'll Be Seeing You" on September 18.

The issue of the POWs is also addressed by other German reports available only as fragments or facsimiles. One of these is the German document KU 3088, generated most likely by the Auswertestelle West center for interrogating Allied airmen in Oberursel. It was found after the war and was later attached to the Missing Air Crew Report 10205, thus remaining outside of the collection in question. KU 3,088 states that Lieutenant Akins' plane was shot down 15 km southeast of Modlin. It also mentions the first and last names of two crew members: Haney and Shook. The document indicates that the Germans captured Haney's "dog tags," while another object revealed the information and address of his wife, Jeanne A. Haney; in addition, there were five cards containing English-to-Russian phrases, one identification card issued to Shook in Pensacola, Florida, and a bicycle card. The exact circumstances in which the Germans obtained these items remain unknown.

The text of another September 1944 German report indicates that radio operator Shook was apprehended by troops from one of the units of the 5th SS Panzer Division. As a result, on September 18 the head-quarters of the 4th SS Panzer Corps in Kazuń dispatched a message to the command of the German 9th Army: "The Wiking Division: ... an American radio operator taken prisoner."[39]

On September 19 the staff of the Luftwaffe (located in Proszkowice at this time) attached to the German 2nd Army claimed: "So far, one wounded pilot, [who is] wounded, is in the hands of the 4th SS Panzer Corps but refuses to reveal information."[40] Was it referring to Shook? It is impossible to determine without further research.

The fate of most of the crew of "I'll Be Seeing You" remains murky. Having used available archival documents and eyewitness testimonies, this work attempts to reconstruct as faithfully as possible the events in question and the fates of the shot-down airmen. In many cases it is simply not possible, however, to provide a final and definitive account of all the various eyewitnesses and documentary reports. Nevertheless, it is possible to provide a best estimation for the reconstruction of the events in question, although we cannot be certain about every aspect of what happened.

The testimonies of the two surviving crew members, Technical Sergeant Shook and Platoon Leader Christy, which were written right after the war, claim that it was probable that all four airmen grouped around the emergency hatch in the tail of the plane managed to bail out. In the case of Sergeant Haney this remains only an assumption. In Sergeant Mac Phee's case, however, the document shows clear indications of certainty that the airman jumped out and could have been killed in a German anti-aircraft barrage.

The belief that more than two airmen bailed out from the aircraft is confirmed by another postwar testimony of Technical Sergeant Shook, who stated that he saw two parachutes (in his 1986 testimony he mentioned only one). At the same time, he also wrote, in a letter to Ryszard Szcześniak in the early 1990s, that he assumed that three or even four people could have conceivably jumped out. Lieutenant Akins' former crew member, Platoon Leader Stefanek, also noticed three falling parachutes.

Taking this into account, it is likely that Shook and Christy were not the only airmen to bail out. This fact was also confirmed by eyewitnesses observing the events from the ground. However, the precise number of airmen who parachuted out remains a mystery.

The Individual Deceased Personnel Files pertaining to the individual crew members are an extremely helpful tool in reconstructing the events of September 18. An examination of the skeletons of the eight men from the perspective of their injuries allows us to divide them into four groups:

1. A large number of injuries: Akins, Shaw, and De Cillis.
2. Above average number of injuries: Berenson and Shimshock.
3. Average number of injuries: Merrill and Mac Phee.
4. Small number of injuries: Haney.

I have created an additional category ("above average") because two airmen, Shimshock and Berenson, sustained skull injuries not observed in the cases of Merrill and Mac Phee.

In the case of, for example, Second Lieutenant Shaw and Lieutenant Akins from the first group, the skeletal injuries are quite serious:

- 2nd Lt. Shaw: multiple fractures of the chest skeletal structure, both shoulder blades, the arm bones, (in the pelvic area) the sacrum, ilium, ischium, the neck of the thigh bone, the thigh bone itself, fibula, a complete fragmentation of the cranium, and missing fragments of the viscerocranium.
- Lt. Akins: multiple fractures of the chest skeletal structure, one shoulder blade, the elbow bone, radial bone, (in the pelvic area) the ilium, sacrum, the neck of the thigh bone, the thigh bone itself, shin bone, a complete fragmentation of the cranium, and missing fragments of the viscerocranium.[41]

The number and type of injuries presented suggest that they were sustained during the course of the crash and constituted the cause of death. Simultaneous cranial, chest-skeletal, and pelvic injuries further suggest that the airmen sustained them while staying at their posts (this pertains particularly to the two mentioned pilots).

In the case of the third group of two airmen mentioned below, the skeletal injuries are much less serious:

- Sergeant Mac Phee: fractures of the elbow bone, both radial bones, and (in the pelvic area) the ischium.
- 2nd Lt. Merrill: fractures of the chest skeletal structure and ischium.

In my view, these kinds of injuries do not suggest a cause of death tied directly to the plane crash but, rather, one external to it.

However, Sergeant Haney, the airman with the least number of injuries, sustained only a fibula fracture to his left leg. Intriguingly, several body parts are missing—the mandible, elbow bone, the right-arm radial bone along with the arm bones, and both rib arches—but this is not an isolated case. As a rule, almost all of the remains are incomplete and missing arm bones (wrist, metacarpal, and phalange bones), feet, mandibles, and kneecaps. The situation is likely the unfortunate result of the dispersal of body parts upon impact and/or the lack of sufficient knowledge and diligence during the 1946 exhumations (this is supported by the mixing-up of the remains revealed by the Americans during the autopsies in Belgium).

An intriguing pattern has emerged from the fact that the clothing of airmen displaying heavy injuries is quite complete, while that of the airmen who sustained light injuries is much less so. Of course, due to individual deviations from this pattern, it is difficult to argue unequivocally for an absolute codependency between both factors. Thus:

- The clothing of Akins and Shaw is largely complete;
- Berenson's, Shimshock's, and Merrill's are characterized by a medium degree of completion;
- Haney's and Mac Phee's clothing is generally incomplete.

However, there are exceptions to the above pattern:

- 2nd Lt. Merrill's injuries and the completeness of his clothing are both average;
- Senior Sergeant De Cillis' body suffered significant injuries but his clothing is mostly incomplete.

The condition of the clothing encountered during the first exhumation, conducted by the Polish Red Cross in November 1946, indicates that both in the case of Lieutenant Akins and Second Lieutenant Shaw we are dealing with largely complete uniforms (excluding the lack of such items as headgear, boots, and gloves typical of all the fallen airmen), whereas the remains of Sergeants Mac Phee and Haney were lacking many important pieces of clothing. This is especially true of Haney, who was buried only in his sweater.

These details may indicate that the bodies of the latter two may have been simply despoiled of their clothing by the locals, which indicates that the uniforms were in decent condition at the moment of death and that they did not perish in a particularly gruesome way. Hence, their deaths most likely occurred not within the aircraft but outside of it.

In the cases of Akins and Shaw, the degree of their injuries probably made it difficult to find items in good condition. Hence, the locals scouring the crash site limited themselves to appropriating only the objects they needed most, i.e., personal property and boots.[42] In this context, we must keep in mind, however, that the postwar protocols listing the clothing items found are not entirely credible. Quite simply, the female employees of the Polish Red Cross preparing these lists in 1946 had no knowledge of the standard-issue clothing worn by the airmen.[43] Most likely they also did not have the benefit of clear guidelines as to the necessary contents of such lists, which often differ from one another substantially.

The eyewitnesses who experienced the downing of the B-17 first hand offer conflicting accounts. One eyewitness account noted two parachutes in the air with one of the crew killed and another captured. While the captured airman is probably Shook or Christy, it is possible that the testimony, offered by a witness from Dziekanów Niemiecki, which is significant, has no connection to either of them. Since two living airmen were seen in Dziekanów Polski and Kiełpin, both Shook and Christy could have been the jumpers who landed on the other side of the Warsaw–Modlin road, i.e., outside the area of the village in question. At the same time, Haney might easily have been the airman captured by the Germans, but the identity of the second airman cannot be ascertained beyond doubt based on this fragmentary testimony.

Another witness saw two airmen not far from one another. Both were killed. One of them was left in his flight suit, while the clothing of the other was removed. This is another testimony from Dziekanów Niemiecki. Provided that it refers to different airmen than the ones seen by the first witness, it would increase the number of sighted airmen bailing out to four and the number of Americans killed to three.

The question of clothing is also confusing, because we cannot be certain exactly what pieces of clothing are referred to and whether the bodies were subjected to looting more than once. Thus, it is not a sufficient clue for identifying specific individuals, for ultimately most of the airmen were stripped of most of their clothing. It can only serve as a basis to make an educated guess as to the identity of the airmen in question. This refers to two pilots, Akins and Shaw, whose uniforms were complete.

A third witness from Dziekanów Niemiecki sighted two airmen. One was killed while descending; another attempted to resist. Seven airmen were buried in a mass grave; one was interred separately. The information regarding an airman killed while descending on a parachute could refer to any of the crew members who managed to bail out (e.g., Sergeant Mac Phee). May we then assume that the second part refers to Sergeant Haney, who, as we know from the extant Polish Red Cross report, was buried separately? Was Haney the American who defended himself or, what is more probable, was he the target of a grenade thrown in his direction, which killed a woman and child, and wounded a German?

A fourth witness from Dąbrowa testified at the end of the war about one captured airman (tall blonde man with a broken leg) who was interrogated by the Germans. He carried a picture of a young girl on his person. Following the interrogation, the airman was executed by the Germans. The exact location is not clearly specified, although it is located close to the crash site near the Warsaw–Modlin road.

Haney's burial in a separate grave may indicate that he was killed in another location or in different circumstances than those of the other men. Perhaps the fragment of the report cited above refers to him. The fact that Haney had dark blonde hair and a broken leg corroborates this. The notes generated by an anthropologist examining his remains also confirm that he was a well-built, muscular man standing at about 176 cm (5 ft 9 in.). He was not the tallest member of the crew, for that distinction belonged to the second pilot, the dark-haired Second Lieutenant Shaw, who stood at 180 cm (5 ft 10 in.). Lower turret gunner, Sergeant Mac Phee, a blonde man of 169 cm (5 ft 6 in.), was not one of the taller crew members.

German reports captured after the war by the Americans indicate that the former seized Haney's and Shook's dog tags. In the case of Haney, the same documents also state that the Nazis came into possession of something referring to his wife and her address. Perhaps this was the photograph mentioned in the report.

A fifth account comes from an individual residing in Kiełpin who reported one airman was killed after a bullet perforated his parachute. According to this testimony, the dead airman was lying next to the main Warsaw–Modlin road. Thus, the number of airmen who jumped out of the bomber is increased to five (including four killed). However, as in other cases, the fragmentary nature of this testimony makes it impossible to determine to which airman it referred. The scope of skeletal injuries may be a misleading indicator here, for some of the injuries could have been sustained on board the aircraft.

Several detailed testimonies boil down to seeing two living airmen spotted, one in Kiełpin, another in Dziekanów Polski, which would indicate two different airmen. These might well have been Christy and Shook.

A seventh set of testimonies features one eyewitness who saw four airmen inside the wreckage of an aircraft which crashed in Dziekanów Leśny, and another witness from the same village transported five or six bodies from the site and laid them next to a dug mass grave.

The total number of airmen in question was seven. This includes five men killed in action (including Haney) and two survivors. But could so many men bail out of the plane? It is not inconceivable that the testimonies from Dziekanów Leśny refer, to some degree, to the same individuals.

The fact that four bodies were seen inside the wreckage limits the number of jumpers to six. Three (including Haney) could have landed in Dziekanów Leśny, one could have ended up alongside the Warsaw–Modlin road, and two could have survived.

We are not certain as to the exact number of bodies gathered and transported to the mass grave, but six is the likely count. This would have included the four bodies inside the wreckage, in addition to two of the airmen who parachuted out over Dziekanów Leśny (one airman, as we know, was buried separately).

Since the sites of the crash and burial were revealed to have been in the same village, Dziekanów Niemiecki, the Americans who were gathering information in August 1947 were unable to reach all of the witnesses of the events of 1944. Most likely they assumed they could not obtain any additional information outside of the area near the sites in question. For this simple reason, the Americans lost an opportunity to acquire more information on the two surviving airmen, the airman killed by the road to Łomianki, the locations in which the individual crew members perished, as well as the gathering and burial of their remains.

The damaged bomber could have been evacuated by six airmen. These were certainly Shook and Christy, most likely Haney, and probably Mac Phee and two more unidentified airmen. It is important to note that the majority of this group consisted of airmen from the rear of the aircraft: the radio operator, two side gunners, and the bottom turret gunner.

An explosion had torn off one of the bomber's wings, rendering the machine uncontrollable as it fell. Combined with centrifugal forces, this prevented the remaining crew members from bailing out. We should assume that, aside from Lieutenant Akins, who was killed as a result of enemy fire, they perished from the injuries sustained at the time or during the crash. This refers to three crew members: Second Lietuenant Shaw and two other airmen, though which two is not entirely certain.

Of the six airmen who bailed out, it is certain that two survived and were captured by the Germans: Shook and Christy. Sergeant Haney was killed either in an unspecified engagement with the Germans or executed by them following an interrogation at the command post of the 19th Panzer Division. The three remaining airmen, Mac Phee, Merrill, and another airman (either Berenson, De Cillis, or Shimshock) perished in the barrage conducted by the Germans from the ground.

Based on available testimonies, it appears that the chief factor determining whether the jumpers survived was their fall site. Two of the airmen, mostly likely Christy and Shook, sighted behind the Warsaw–Modlin road, survived. One landed in arable fields completely devoid of people and buildings, while another fell near a village 4 km away from the main crash site. The tragedy of the remaining airmen was that they practically dropped on the heads of disoriented German soldiers of the 27th Panzer Regiment deployed in Dziekanów Niemiecki who were shooting blindly into the air.

Given the number of bullets fired into Shimshock's body, as well as information regarding the causes of death of the other parachuting crew members, it is important to recall tests conducted by the British during the war. These demonstrated that a well-trained marksman shooting from a distance of 135 m was capable of striking a parachutist only once for every 300 bullets fired. When the firing distance was doubled to 270 m, the ratio was one hit per 1,700 bullets. This radical experiment points to one of two things. Either Shimshock died after being shot at by a large number of marksmen firing a great quantity of ammunition or he was shot at from close range.

Unfortunately, it not possible to clarify the suggestion by witness Klemens Bogurat that one of the airmen was captured on the other side of the Vistula River, in Rajszew, where a German anti-aircraft battery was deployed.

Many publications, both scholarly books and popular articles, on the fate of the crew of "I'll Be Seeing You," promote the unsubstantiated claim that the American airman executed by the Germans in modern-day Dziekanów Leśny or its environs was tail gunner Shimshock. The origins of this oft-repeated version of events remain a mystery. An assessment of the facts seems to point to the improbability of this narrative thread. This claim is debunked by:

1. The established facts about Sergeant Haney, i.e., his individual burial, the confirmation of his physical description by a Home Army report, the capture of his dog tag and another piece of personal property by the Germans, and his broken leg.

2. The number and type of skeletal injuries to Sergeant Shimshock's body, i.e., fractures of the right clavicle, arm bone, radial bone, both thigh bones, and the fibula, in addition to cranial injuries, including a missing occipital bone and a fragment of the parietal bone.
3. The fact that Sergeant Shimshock's personal property remained on or nearby his person. He could have been found somewhat later (after the initial wave of looting subsided) or perished in another location (e.g., the single airman near the road in testimony no. 5) than that of the remaining airmen, who, as all the testimonies indicate, were despoiled of their property. The case of the other men suggests that both the survivors and the fallen (the pilots: Arrants, Vigna, and Peters) were robbed of their property by German soldiers, who treated it as valuable plunder or nice souvenirs.
4. Sergeant Shimshock's physical description: dark hair color, 170 cm tall.

On August 7, 1989 documents pertaining to a case opened by the District Commission for Researching Nazi Crimes in Warsaw in September 1988, into the matter of "the murder of eight American airmen from among the crew of a shot-down transport plane carrying aid to Insurgent Warsaw in mid-September 1944 in the area of the village of Dziekanów Leśny (the Warsaw County)," were transferred to the Center for Research into National Socialist Crimes in Ludwigsburg (Germany) for the purpose of conducting a criminal investigation.[44]

As the authors have established, the documents were then subsequently transferred to the prosecutor's office in Bremen, which was in charge of investigating German crimes during the Warsaw Uprising. In 1994 the case was closed since the documents offered no new leads. Thus, the motion to dismiss the case from February 19, 1982 was upheld. The decision was justified by the argument that numerous German units were deployed in the area in which the events in question occurred, which meant a very large pool of potential suspects. Thus, it was impossible to identify specific culprits.[45]

Since the case is classified as a war crime in Poland, however, it is not subject to the statute of limitations. Given the sluggish manner in which the proper institutions have approached the case, coupled with the fact that the direct participants and witnesses have passed away with time, it appears that clarifying the matter based on a legal foundation (rather than individual research) will be impossible.

It is important to point out that in such cases the German and Polish approaches differ substantially. Both sides agree that a war crime has occurred whenever a particular individual is killed outside of the context of combat in wartime. However, in the case of Poland such killings are never subject to the statute of limitations, while in Germany only murders are not subject to it.[46] Thus, it is always necessary to prove that a particular killing was a murder. In light of existing German laws, a murder occurs only when a homicide was the effect of a ruse or racial hatred, was accompanied by particular cruelty, and the culprit was motivated by blood-lust, greed, or other ulterior motives.

In light of the above, one may speculate whether the death of the crew members of "I'll Be Seeing You," who managed to bail out of the bomber and were shot down by German soldiers, most likely the troops of the 27th Panzer Regiment of the 19th Panzer Division, would have been classified by the Germans as a homicide resulting from wartime combat, thereby not qualifying as a war crime. In the latter case, the question remains open whether the above events would later qualify as murders, which are not subject to the statute of limitations, or killings. In our view, only the case of the single airman captured and executed immediately following his interrogation could be presumably classified as a murder. This could happen only if the prosecution managed to obtain the testimonies of the culprits and eyewitnesses, and to prove beyond reasonable doubt that the criteria for qualifying the killing as a murder were satisfied.

Given the above conditions, not to mention problems in reaching the culprits, it is doubtful that a verdict would have been passed and the guilty punished at all.

Finally, it has been impossible to determine the location and circumstances of the capture of gunner Christy. Thus, there is the question of why he reached the Gross Tychow POW camp so long after his capture (one month afterward), while Shook reached his destination in five to six days. What happened to him during this time remains a mystery.

None of the available reports or documents contain his name or any information connected to him. Given the postwar fate of American POWs in Germany, it is likely that Christy was evacuated via one of the evacuation camps located in northern France, i.e., the so-called "Cigarette Camps" in the Le Havre–Rouen area or the "City Camps" located in the vicinity of Reims.

CHAPTER 7

After the Airdrop

Within hours of the American parachutes landing in Warsaw, observers on all sides of the conflict tried to assess what had happened and how it would affect the course of the war. Poles, Germans, Americans, and Soviets tried to peer through the fog of war in the days that followed, not only to better understand the results of *Frantic 7* but in some cases to turn either the success or failure of the mission into useful propaganda.

Operation *Frantic 7* found its way into nearly all of the underground publications appearing in the city at the time, regardless of the political orientation of the periodicals. The first batch of articles on the subject, appearing several hours after the operation, were hastily edited communiqués published in the heat of the fighting taking place around the city.

For example, *Insurgent News* published an article titled "The Allies over Warsaw":

> Today, at 1345 h, many squadrons of long-awaited Allied planes appeared over Warsaw and dropped a large number of containers with ammunition, weapons, and food. In spite of very heavy German artillery fire, as far as we managed to notice, all the planes departed to the east. The details of this large-scale assistance are still not known.[1]

Leftist and pro-Soviet publications tried to claim the airdrop was assistance from the Soviets. Both the socialist Bulletin of District IV of the Polish Socialist Party and the Warsaw District of the Polish Socialist Party, and the publication of the Polish Syndicalist Union and the Syndicalist Insurgent Alliance, *Sprawa* [The Cause], fed their readers the false information that the airlift was the work of the Soviets. One publication noted: "Today, at 1345 h, the Soviet forces dropped supplies over the area of Żoliborz. The local population observed the landing of the supplies with great joy."[2] Another reported that "Today, in the afternoon hours, the Soviet air force parachuted large amounts of supplies over the Warsaw area. So far we have no more information on the character of the above action."[3]

As the dust settled, later articles elaborated on previously published information, provided new details of the operation, and verified the numbers of aircraft and containers captured by the insurgents. The publications emphasized the enthusiastic reactions of Warsaw's inhabitants and improved morale, particularly in the northern part of the City Center, where the largest number of containers were seized. In spite of the fact that an estimated lion's share (about 80%) of the supplies fell into German hands, the assistance was nevertheless considered the most significant the insurgents had heretofore received.

Biuletyn Krajowy [The National Bulletin] published a communiqué of the insurgent Polish Telegraphic Agency (PAT) titled "American Assistance for Warsaw":

> Warsaw, September 18, PAT. The official circles have communicated that the Allied airlift expedition to assist Warsaw had been planned for several days, but was called off several times due to inclement weather. It first took place on Monday, when the conditions improved sufficiently. Tens of American "Flying Fortresses" flew over Warsaw during the afternoon hours and dropped a large number of parachutes with supplies. The "Flying Fortresses" landed on Russian airfields. We may assume that this was the first phase of assistance provided by the U.S. air force. Soon other airlifts will occur. German anti-aircraft artillery opened a frenzied fire against the American planes, but it ended up becoming a disorderly shoot-out.

The following day, *Biuletyn Informacyjny* noted:

> Yesterday, at about 1400 h, large squadrons of American planes, over 70 in total, appeared over Warsaw. The aircraft dropped several hundred containers on parachutes. The sight of the mighty air flotilla of our allies bringing aid for Warsaw produced great enthusiasm among the inhabitants. Unfortunately, much of the containers, which were dropped from high altitudes, fell in areas held by the Germans. As the Americans passed above Warsaw, Soviet bombers also attacked the area of the Saxon Gardens.[4]

Another insurgent publication wrote:

> London communicates the following about yesterday's Anglo-Saxon flight over Warsaw: heavy American bombers from bases in Great Britain flew over Warsaw, where they dropped weapons, ammunition, and food, and subsequently departed for bases in Russia. This was the first instance of weapons delivered by air directly from Great Britain.
>
> The bombers were protected by a great number of fighters. They did not encounter enemy opposition along the way. They found themselves fired upon by anti-aircraft artillery above Warsaw, which was at times weak, and at times intensive.
>
> The fighters did not continue on to the Russian bases but returned to England. As they [the fighters] returned home, they shot-down four German fighters in dog fights and bombed ground targets in Germany destroying three enemy planes on the ground.
>
> Understandably, given the complicated course of the front line in Warsaw, some of the dropped containers fell into German hands. Even so, the supplies that the Home Army managed to capture constitute a desirable and significant boon.[5]

Robotnik [The Worker], the flagship publication of the Polish Socialist Party, commented:

> Warsaw experienced quite an uplifting moment yesterday. At about two o'clock [in the afternoon] squadrons of four-engine bombers in groups of 12 appeared over the city flying in from the southwest. In total, observers counted about 100 planes, which dropped hundreds of containers on parachutes from a rather high altitude.
>
> German anti-aircraft and heavy machine gun fire did not manage to hinder the airdrop or to seriously damage the falling parachutes. It was inevitable, given the situation in which Polish and German positions have cut the city up into a veritable chessboard, that some of the containers fell into German-held territory. However, it is indubitable that whatever fell into our hands will seriously reinforce our units and provide us with renewed strength and energy to continue the fight.[6]

Among the many voices there was no shortage of less enthusiastic assessments of the American mission and its effects, particularly from communists oriented toward the Soviet Union. Even the Head Commander of the Home Army, General "Bór" Komorowski, was not spared bitter accusations of conducting false and unrealistic propaganda. The pro-Soviet *Armia Ludowa* stated:

At 2315 h London issued the following statement: "Numerous formations of American Flying Fortresses dropped weapons and supplies for Warsaw during their flight from England to Russia. The formations were shielded by great squadrons of fighters, which returned to England." We are grateful to our Western allies for the assistance provided.

At the same time, we would like to appeal to Gen. Bór to refrain from sending overly optimistic messages to London. The Allied airmen would then be more knowledgeable about the real situation in Warsaw, which would allow them to conduct the drops in such a manner that the weapons would actually fall into our hands, and not those of the Germans.[7]

The same periodical continued in a similar vein the following day:

On the 18th of this month, several dozens of American bombers dropped weapons, ammunition, and food over Warsaw. The sight certainly made an impression. In broad daylight tens of parachutes opened up above the city generating enthusiasm among the population.

This fact has been used by the émigré camp [i.e., non-communists] and its branches in Poland to carry out a broad propaganda campaign. A deluge of long and enthusiastic articles, telegrams, and expressions of gratitude, contrasting sharply with shameful and caustic comments on Soviet help, has followed. ... Gen. Bór's enthusiastic dispatches probably forgot to mention that the lion's share of the airdropped supplies fell into German hands.

The supporters of the émigrés were not concerned about the quantity [of captured supplies], for they were concerned not about assistance, but about propaganda.[8]

On September 19, current events commentator Jan Gor discussed the airdrop in the daily "Day of Combat" (*Dzień walki*) news cycle preceding the evening programming of the insurgent radio station "Lightning" (*Błyskawica*):

Yesterday, we had Anglo-Saxon airdrops during the day. The colorful parachutes looked beautiful in the sky. After a long hiatus, we once again registered help from our Western allies.

Nevertheless, the [current] reality is so cruel that the joy generated by the assistance is muffled by the macabre of the smoldering ruins, the musty cellars which have become the homes of hundreds of thousands of people deprived of a roof over their heads, the now universal hunger, the unbearable lack of water, [and] the increasingly gnawing cold.[9]

During a review of the Polish press on the same program, excerpts from newspapers appearing in insurgent Warsaw were read out.

> Yesterday's passage over Warsaw of a significant number of American four-engine planes dropping assistance in the form of ammunition and food awakened the spontaneous enthusiasm of the suffering population.
>
> This direct Anglo-Saxon aid, declared more than a week ago, further breaks our long isolation. ... We expect that the Anglo-Saxon assistance provided to us yesterday will not be a merely tentative and one-time measure, but a systematic one, [and] that it will be organized in the proper way, so as to avoid some of the tactical errors of the first attempt during the succeeding ones. So far, it suffices that the passage of the air armada over the city yesterday demonstrated the real voice of England and America: We are with you.[10]

Another periodical read over the air stated:

> Following 7 weeks of fighting we have finally received the first long-awaited serious assistance from England, which we have been demanding from the inception of the uprising. We will not once again question why this aid, which we had a right to expect right away after the insurrection was launched, arrived only today. Yesterday's operation above Warsaw by the Anglo-Saxon air force was a great demonstration of our Western allies' air power and their ability to bring us effective help. At the same time, it proved that the initial difficulties in our [Polish-Allied] cooperation in this regard have been finally overcome and that the Anglo-Saxons will actively intervene in matters relevant for the uprising in the future. That is how fighting Warsaw understood yesterday's airlift by the Anglo-Saxon air force.
>
> We are convinced that, from the military point of view, they [the airdrops] presage additional and more effective aid operations, and that, politically, they are an expression of the will of England and the United States to participate actively in the shaping of a future Poland.[11]

The radio hosts then concluded their review of the press by inserting a dramatic commentary of their own which clearly expressed fears for the fate of the city and its inhabitants:

> The mood of the Warsaw press is an expression of the mood of Warsaw's inhabitants today. Whenever a man exhausted by thirst receives a drop of water, he is grateful for the temporary relief. We are grateful. Yet, tomorrow's events will show how much of a discrepancy actually exists between our mood and the reality.[12]

Soon thereafter, two of the few Polish-language collaborationist outlets published by the Germans, *Nowy Kurier Warszawski*, which was published in Łódź, and *Goniec Krakowski*, chimed in as well on the airlift of September 18. On September 24, *Nowy Kurier Warszawski* published an article titled "Roosevelt Sent Cans of Rotten Meat and Dog Biscuits to the Insurgents in Warsaw: New Evidence of Anglo-Saxon Friendship." Given that the containers fell in areas long held by the Germans, the author claimed that the plan of the expedition had been based on out-of-date information from 6 weeks prior to the expedition's departure. He also claimed that the boxes captured by the Germans contained "Armour's Star" brand canned meat produced in Brazil. In addition, the author claimed that some of the cans contained either dampened or completely rotten meat. The crates also held crackers, which the collaborationist pundit described as "dog biscuits with which Roosevelt intends to feed 'liberated Europe.'"[13]

The author concluded his article in the sarcastic style defining his piece throughout: "Perhaps, unbeknownst to us, the Warsaw insurgents have used dogs as auxiliaries in combat? Perhaps they formed entire units from loyal dogs and it was for these canine corps that America dropped the necessary food?"

Another article, published on September 30 in the collaborationist *Goniec Krakowski*, titled "The Allies' Help Lasted for Only Three Days," was somewhat more reserved. Citing a Polish-language radio message from Stockholm in Sweden, intercepted by the Germans, the author wrote:

> The aid the Warsaw insurgents received is insufficient. In many cases the airdropped food is inedible. The assistance supplied by the American airplanes lasted for only 3 days. According to human estimates [sic], the insurgents cannot hold out for much longer. If nothing happens, the last drop of blood will soon flow.

Aside from the popular reaction in the Polish underground press, the Polish Home Army also assessed the airdrop and its results. On September 18 at 2200 h, the commander of the Warsaw District, Col. Antoni Chruściel "Monter," submitted a report to the command of the Home Army (AK) informing his superiors of the supply drop conducted on that day. In the same report he also estimated that the insurgents captured about 80 containers in the City Center. He pointed out, however, that he had not yet received reports from Żoliborz and Mokotów.

The following day, September 19, a dispatch was sent by the commander of the Home Army to the staff of the Commander-in-Chief in London:

About 100 containers fell in the City Center, most of which was arms. Currently there are no reports from Mokotów, Żoliborz, and Czerniaków. The operations defects of the drops were:

1. A high altitude, the parachutes descended through several layers of different wind currents.
2. Direct drops from the course on which the aircraft were traveling without identifying the drop signals, hence the low drop accuracy.
3. Drops using large teams made it difficult to maneuver and resulted in uneven coverage. Further data will be sent afterward.[14]

The missing report of the commander of the Mokotów grouping, Lt. Col. Józef Rokicki "Karol," reached the district commander already on September 18: "Most of the drop at 1400 h fell in enemy territory or in no-man's land from [the] east and will only be captured at night. So far, 12 automatic pistols and 2,400 9 mm ammunition."[15]

In the case of Żoliborz, information about the American airdrop arrived only on September 20. On the same day, the commander of the Żoliborz district, Lt. Col. Mieczysław Niedzielski "Żywiciel," reported to the district commander: "The daytime drops on September 18 were captured by the enemy."[16]

Also on September 20, Department VI of the staff of the Commander-in-Chief assessed the effects of the expedition. The document contained not only information regarding the quantity of airdropped supplies, but also the number of captured containers and data about the sites where these landed. In general, 1,250 containers (each containing about 100 net kg of equipment) were dropped over Warsaw, with 750 on the City Center, 200 on Żoliborz, and 300 on Mokotów.

According to reports gathered until September 20, the results of the drops were as follows:

1. Żoliborz: Objective missed; the containers landed in the area of Góry Szwedzkie behind enemy positions, [and] 4 km to the west of the target.17

2. City Center: Most of the drop fell to the northeast of the objective. Containers were captured in the northern part of the area. Some of the containers, probably from this group, landed in the Vistula or in Praga.

3. Mokotów: The center of the drops was concentrated about 2 km to the east of the objective, [and] the containers fell in the no-man's land in front of our units. A nighttime operation to recover them was planned. There are no further details at this moment. Up to this point, the seizure of about 130 containers has been officially confirmed, i.e., over 10% of the entirety and over 17% [of the containers] dropped over the City Center.[18]

Two days later, on the basis of further reports flowing into London on September 21 and 22, the previous balance sheet was updated to include the capture of 228 containers (including 77 captured in combat). The reports noted that the location of 32 had been ascertained, but whose capture requires additional fighting. Another 28 containers were damaged on landing as a result of the burning of the parachutes by incendiary projectiles fired by the enemy. Altogether, 288 containers in total were accounted for by the AK.[19]

The remainder of the report is dedicated to musings on additional containers, which could have been captured by the civilian population or by individual units without notifying the insurrectionary authorities. These were assessed at around 100 containers. According to the author of the report, the total number of captured containers was thus 388, constituting 37% of the entire drop. We are not told, however, about the fate of the 32 containers which had to be fought over, or the 28 crates damaged as a result of incendiary shells striking their parachutes.

The lack of precise data makes it impossible to determine the exact number of containers loaded onto each aircraft. Detailed information is also missing about the quantity of the early airdrop in the Modlin–Dziekanów Niemiecki area, the number of containers dropped over the city of Warsaw itself, and the number of crates captured by the insurgents and civilians.[20] Thus, it is impossible to determine precisely how many containers were retrieved. However, it is possible to assume that only about 28% of the airdrop was captured in the areas held by the insurgents. Thus, the remainder either fell into German hands, could not be retrieved because of Nazi fire, fell into the river, or landed on the Soviet-controlled side of the city in Praga.

Moreover, the Americans themselves assessed the expedition of September 18 in two diametrically different ways. The official version was reflected in statements issued immediately after the airlift and, by extension, found its way into the press coverage at the time. The unofficial version consisted of strictly military analyses generated later on. These were classified as "confidential," "restricted," or "secret," and thus unavailable to public opinion. In the case of the former, the effects of the airdrop are themselves not assessed.[21] The authors of the communiqués and the articles based on them generally limit themselves to a general description of the course of the mission, sometimes supplemented by the intensely emotional testimonies of some of the airmen, and the numbers of machines shot-down and lost. Accordingly, the expedition is always presented in a positive light and as a success with minimal losses incurred.

An article published in the Polish London-based *Dziennik Polski i Dziennik Żołnierza* (The Polish Daily and the Soldier's Daily) on September 20, titled "A Great Success: The Expedition of Flying Fortresses over Warsaw Suffers Only Small Losses," was written in the same spirit. The article also mentioned the communiqué of the headquarters of the American strategic air force in Europe published on September 18 at 2220 h:

> The Flying Fortresses of the 8th American Air Force dropped supplies for Polish units in Warsaw today. The bombers then flew to bases in Russia. Mustangs belonging to the 8th Air Force Command escorted the bombers. Some of the fighters went on to Warsaw and continued their flight to bases in Russia, while the rest turned back near the Polish frontier and returned to bases in England. The anti-aircraft artillery fire was moderately heavy, but sometimes intensive, but no German fighters attacked the bombers. Our fighters which returned to England encountered a small number of enemy aircraft and shot down four in aerial combat. They also destroyed three more on airfields in Germany. All of the fighters which belonged to the formation which returned to England came back intact. No information has so far arrived regarding the bombers and fighters which continued on to Russia.

The communiqué announced by the headquarters of the American tactical air force Eastern Command states that Soviet fighters supported the American formation above the Warsaw area and above Soviet territory. The American losses amounted to two bombers and two Mustangs. Four enemy fighters were destroyed.

The communiqué also states that the mission was highly successful and the losses insignificant given the unfavorable atmospheric conditions over a part of the route, the anti-aircraft fire encountered, and the altitude which was a few thousand feet lower than in normal bombing missions.[22]

In the second, unofficial case, the reports speak of the complete success of the mission, but, simultaneously, point out that it is difficult to speak of concrete results since the crews were unable to establish the final landing sites of most of the drop. They state that, in their view, only about half the supplies fell within the city limits. As the dust settled and time passed, this assessment became much more unfavorable and the new negative evaluation would soon become the main argument against the decision to repeat the airlift. According to assessments passed on to headquarters by the individual bomber groups, the losses were as follows:

- 95th Bomber Group: Six of the 18 that had been hit during the operation were seriously damaged.[23]
- 100th Bomber Group: No serious losses; one damaged aircraft remained in the USSR.
- 390th Bomber Group: One aircraft irretrievably lost, seven heavily damaged,[24] 24 aircraft damaged by enemy Flak fire landed successfully in Poltava and Mirgorod.
- In addition, a few Mustangs of the 355th Fighter Group escorting the expedition were damaged in addition to the three destroyed.[25]

Further, the evaluation of the effects of the airlift is negative in these reports. A telling example was Major General Anderson's "Memorandum: Warsaw Assistance Operation."[26] Dated October 15, the memorandum was addressed to the commander of the USSTAF, Lieutenant General Spaatz. Anderson wrote that, contrary to information obtained from Polish military circles in London as to the alleged practical nonexistence of German anti-aircraft defenses around the city, these turned out not to deviate from the norm. This forced the Allies to conduct the drops from an altitude above 10,000 ft. The great distance, the high level of enemy activity, and the fact that the crew were not prepared for this kind of mission, meant that in the future Allied commanders should take into account that the operation "would be much more than just a noble gesture" when deciding to implement it.

Anderson stated that the crews practiced carrying out their assignment from the planned altitude. The test showed that, even if the mission was carried out according to plan, it would have been unrealistic to expect that more than 20% of the containers would fall within the areas of the city controlled by the insurgents.

As time would prove, these predictions eventually became reality. According to the author of the report, it is safe to conclude that only a small portion of the drop actually fell into Polish hands, perhaps 25 or 30% of the containers. More than half of the airlifted supplies were captured by the Germans or the Soviets holding the eastern part of the city.

Major General Anderson also pointed out that the price of Operation *Frantic* 7 was the loss of two bombers and two fighters (in reality: one bomber and three fighters) and the unavailability of 105 bombers and 62 fighters for other missions for over a week.[27]

The additional cost, in Anderson's view, was the loss of prestige in Soviet eyes, and the fact that any credit the Americans may have gained was ultimately nullified by the bitterness stemming from the fact that the Western Allies were unable to save "neither their army, nor their city, nor many additional human lives."

German documents and American testimonies show that the planners of the expedition chose a particularly unsuitable approach path toward the target. Aside from the significant problems in locating the IP by the various elements of the expedition, it was also an unfortunate coincidence that the entire bombing course (and later the lone flight of Lieutenant Akins' plane), beginning from Modlin and terminating over Dziekanów Niemiecki and Dąbrowa, ran over a territory filled with heavy 88 mm German anti-aircraft gun batteries whose range overlapped.[28] Another factor was the direct proximity of as many as four airfields from which German fighters could operate.

It is possible that the other approach paths, including the southwestern one suggested by the lead navigator of the 390th Bomber Group's Wing C, Lt. John B. Wey, would have been more advantageous but this cannot be confirmed with any certainty. The northern path meant flying over the Vistula–Narew river fork heavily defended by the Germans, in addition to the Modlin Fortress, the river crossings existing in the area, and the direct neighborhood of the frontline in the Jabłonna area. However, the southern approach entailed flying over the Vistula, which constituted the frontline, in addition to the heavily defended area near the Soviet-held Warka-Magnuszew Bridgehead.

The Germans were not the only force observing the airdrop. On September 14, 1944, units of the 1st Soviet Belarusian Front, including the 1st Tadeusz Kościuszko Infantry Division detached from the 1st Army of the Soviet-controlled Polish military, captured the eastern bank of the Vistula near Warsaw. By evening on the following day, the remaining units constituting the ethnically Polish 1st Army were redeployed to the Praga district from defensive positions they had been holding in the northern part of the Warka-Magnuszew Bridgehead. The units now occupied the positions of the Soviet units which had participated in the fighting for Praga and the 1st Kościuszko Infantry Division. As a result of this shift, the 2nd Jarosław Henryk Dąbrowski Infantry Division was deployed in the Bródno area across the river from Żoliborz. South of it, the line down to the detonated Poniatowski Bridge was manned by the 1st Cavalry Brigade, while the 3rd Romuald Traugutt Infantry Division occupied the Saska Kępa district around Czerniaków.

Surviving documents prove that the Soviet units comprising the 1st Belarusian Front received advanced warning of the planned American airlift. The units of the 1st Army of the Polish military were informed already on September 13. On the same day, at 2245 h, they received Order no. 0061, issued by the Chief of the Operational Department of the Staff, Col. Dionizy Surżyc, which stated:

> At around 1400 h on September 14, 1944 American airplanes on a combat mission will pass over the city of Warsaw in the direction of the city of Poltava

consisting of 100 "Flying Fortress" bombers escorted by 64 "Moustang" [sic] fighters. The Army commander has ordered that, immediately on receiving this order, all our units be issued orders to secure the transit of the above mentioned planes. The identifying markings of the plane are in accordance with the previous order issued to you in the month of June 1944.[29]

As mentioned earlier, the expedition scheduled for September 14 was called off due to the inclement weather over Britain. The other surviving documents pertain to September 18. Two reports generated by the 2nd Infantry Division offer only general observations. Combat Report no. 337 of the 2nd Infantry Division for September 18, 1944 (Grochów) stated: "At 1500 h [Moscow time] a group of American airplanes of the 'Flying Fortress' type passed above the city of Warsaw, which dropped a large number of parachutes above the insurgent-held territory, most of which landed in the center of the Żoliborz District."[30] A report by the Senior Instructor of the 2nd Infantry Division, Second Lieutenant Fritzhand, dated September 19, 1944, and addressed to the division's Deputy Commander for Political-Behavioral (i.e., Propaganda) stated: "During our sojourn in the battalion, four-engine aircraft dropped what was most likely arms and food for the insurgents. However, the soldiers disseminated the version that 'paratroopers from England' were dropped."[31]

The false theme of Allied paratroopers spread by the soldiers also found its way into a staff report of the 1st Cavalry Brigade to the commander of the 1st Army of the Polish communist military, Gen. Zygmunt Berling. The report stated: "At 1430 h an airdrop of about 300–500 parachutes was conducted over the southern and southwestern district of Warsaw. Following the landing of the airdrop we could hear intensified activity and automatic weapons fire."[32]

A report prepared on September 20 by the Chief-of-Staff of the 1st Belarusian Front, Colonel General Malinin, and addressed to the Chief-of-Staff of the Soviet Army, showed how the Soviets viewed the airlift and its effectiveness:

September 18, 1944: between 15:20 and 15:25, 100 "Super Fortresses" [sic] escorted by "Mustang" fighters passed over Warsaw. The airplanes flew in tight formation in groups of 12–15 planes with only small gaps between the groups.

As they passed over the Warsaw area at an altitude below 4,500 m, the planes dropped supplies. Observation from the eastern bank of the Vistula had determined that about 230 parachutes with supplies fell most likely in the following areas:

- The first group in the area delineated from the north by Żoliborska Street, to the west by Dzika, to the south by Senatorska Street, and to the east by the Vistula River;

- The second group in the race track area;

- The third group in the area of southwestern Żoliborz, delineated from the north by Krasińskiego [Street], to the west by Elbląska, to the south by Gęsia, and to the east by Dzika in the southwestern edge of Żoliborz;

- The fourth group in the area delineated by Królewska [Street] to the north, Sosnowa to the west, Piękna to the south, and Solec to the east.

Because the drops were conducted from a great altitude, the distribution of the parachutes became increasingly dispersed as they descended, causing the supplies to fall over a very large area, including areas outside of the city limits.

For example, a drop of 10 parachutes thus fell in the area of Ruda, 5 km to the west of Mińsk Mazowiecki. One container crashed. Inside there were artillery shells, rifles, and automatic and regular pistols. These supplies were captured and secured.

A comparison of the available data about insurgent-held territory in Warsaw with data obtained by observing the airdrops [shows] it is safe to assume that these drops fell outside of the areas held by the insurgents.

People escaping from Warsaw said that all the supplies dropped on September 18, 1944 within the area of the city have fallen into enemy hands. Thus, in practice, the English and the Americans have armed the Germans, not the insurgents. As the American aircraft appeared over Warsaw, four enemy medium-caliber anti-aircraft batteries opened fire, as a result of which two aircraft were shot down, one "Flying Fortress" and one "Mustang," which crashed in enemy-held territory.[33]

On September 22, 1944, Lieutenant General Tielegina, a member of the 1st Belarusian Front's War Council, reported to the head of the Red Army's Head Political Department:

While dropping supplies, the American and English air force is not, in fact, helping the insurgents, but arming the Germans. Following special observation by storm and fighter aircraft above Warsaw as well as ground [observation] posts, it was noted that on September 18, during the hours of 15:20–15:25, one hundred "Super Fortresses" [sic] dropped 1,000 containers with parachutes in the Warsaw area, of which 21 fell in areas occupied by the insurgents, 19 fell in areas held by our units, and 960 fell into German hands. Drops were conducted from an altitude of 4,000 m, from which it is practically impossible to drop supplies over an area held by insurgents.

One "Super Fortress" dropped 10 containers in the area of Mińsk Mazowiecki, i.e., about 40 km from Warsaw. While examining the contents of the drop we found: explosives, a mortar with 20 shells, two machine guns with bullets, 10 automatic pistols and 3 [regular] pistols, automatic pistol bullets, 4 grenades, Bichford rope, [and] packages with food (100 small cans of meat, 6 boxes of biscuits, crackers, and chocolate). The weaponry was damaged during the impact.[34]

The combat history of the 16th Soviet Air Army, which supported the forces of the 1st Belarusian Front, dated October 12, 1944, offers additional details. Titled "The Activities of the Air Forces of the 16th Air Army," the survey addresses such issues as: cooperation with the insurgents, the rule of communicating with them, and the logistical organization of Soviet airdrops begun on September 14. To a degree, it also mentions the earlier British airdrops and the subsequent American airlift.

According to this document, the Soviets earmarked the aircraft of the 6th Fighter Air Force Corps, consisting of the 286th, 28th, and 2nd Fighter Regiments, for cooperation with the Americans. These Soviet aircraft flew above the Allied formations at an altitude of 1,500–3,800 ft and "protected and escorted them to the Warsaw area."[35] Simultaneously, aircraft of the 2nd Guards Storm Air Force Division were also operating at the height of 300–500 m above the city and photographing the area.

Unfortunately, the above document fails to mention precisely at what point the Soviet planes accompanied the air armada, nor does it reveal whether the Soviet fighters engaged actively in protecting the expedition from German fighter attacks. Since American testimonies stated that the American bombers traveled at altitudes from 4,200 to 5,500 m, the presence of Soviets (flying below the formation and not above it, as the Soviet summary claims) would not have gone unnoticed. The only known testimony that mentions Soviet assistance in the air was written by Lt. Art H. Juhlin. He was the lead navigator onboard the aircraft "Andy's Dandies" (418th Squadron, piloted by Donald A. Jones), which belonged to the 100th Bombing Group's Wing C. Juhlin recalls that Soviet fighters took over the escorting duties over the objective and accompanied the bombers to their Soviet bases.

Other American documents, including reports and testimonies by fighter and bomber pilots, mention nothing about the presence of Soviet planes. This indicates that the Soviets may have played a very limited role.

The description of the American expedition of September 18 quoted below is a fragment of the Red Air Force document. According to the annotations, it was generated by the Soviets on the basis of reports by the 16th Soviet Air Army's airmen as well as its ground and artillery observers.

> 18.9.44, during the hours of 14:50–15:10, eight groups of 12 "Flying Fortresses" each, escorted by Mustang fighters, about six groups of eight planes each appeared above Warsaw from the West, [the Flying Fortress groups] flying at large distances of 1,500 m from one another at an altitude of 4,000 m.
>
> The Flying Fortresses flew in tight formation of wedged groups of 12 planes. The Mustang fighters flew in groups of eight and separate pairs in between the groups of bombers.
>
> While approaching the city of Warsaw, four groups of Flying Fortresses flew toward the northern part of the city, and four [other] groups toward the southern [part].
>
> The dropping of the cargo followed the lead of the head of each group. Parachutes of various sizes and colors were observed in the air. Seventy percent of the loads dropped over the northern part of the city of Warsaw fell in the areas of Buraków, Parysów, and Izabelin, while 30% fell in the area of Marymont. Individual containers with parachutes landed on the eastern bank of the Vistula [about] 800–1,000 m to the south of Pelcowizna.
>
> Sixty percent of the supplies dropped over the southern part of the city fell in the western part of the City Center and about 20% in the area of Mokotów. Individual cargos on parachutes landed about 400–600 m from Czerniaków Lake.
>
> One Super Fortress plane dropped 10 containers on parachutes in the area of Ruda (4 km to the west of Mińsk Mazowiecki), i.e., 40 km away from the center of the city of Warsaw in Red Army-held territory.

According to storm aircraft crews serving as observers and flying at altitudes of 300–500 m, the following numbers of containers with parachutes were dropped in the following areas held by the insurgents: five parachutes in the area of Graniczna, [and] Królewska Streets; three parachutes in the area of Aleje Jerozolimskie, Marszałkowska, Nowogrodzka, [and] Krucza Streets; seven parachutes in the area of Wilanowska, [and] Czerniakowska Streets; one parachute in the area of Mokotów.

In general, probably no more than 21 containers with parachutes fell in insurgent-held territory.

According to all observers, both ground-based and airborne, the Flying Fortress airplanes dropped about 1,000 containers with parachutes from various altitudes over the city of Warsaw. About 21 of those containers with parachutes fell in insurgent-held areas, if we are to consider the information coming from these areas as credible. Of the remaining approximate number of more than 980 containers, about 20 fell in areas held by the Red Army and over 960 fell into German hands.

As the Flying Fortress planes dropped their cargo, the enemy's anti-aircraft fire, including small-caliber [anti-aircraft artillery] fire, was strong. The groups of aircraft above the northern part of the city of Warsaw received the most intensive fire.

According to data provided by our anti-aircraft defense units and observers, the enemy's anti-aircraft artillery shot down two Flying Fortresses. One of them disintegrated in the air. One Flying Fortress was damaged by a Focke Wulf 190 [German fighter] and was forced to conduct an emergency landing at the airfield in Brest. The crew survived and suffered no serious injuries. The aircraft's tail-plane was damaged. Following on-the-spot repairs, the machine flew on to Poltava airbase. The crew [consisted of]: the commander, a young lieutenant by the name of Jonston [sic]; the second pilot, the young lieutenant Robinson; (the bomb gunner [sic: bombardier]), the young lieutenant Opnei; the navigator, the young lieutenant Lash; the radio operator, Sergeant Parks; the mechanic, Sergeant Chardick; the gunners, "Sergeants" [sic] Marshall, Kelly, [and] Loumen. In addition, the crew was also assigned a photographer during the operation, a "Sergeant" Kesanto.[36] His tasks included photographing important German facilities and the course of the airdrop for the Poles in Warsaw. He failed to take almost any pictures because he did not notice note-worthy facilities and was unable to further carry out his assignment because his plane was fired upon during the approach to Warsaw.[37]

The Soviet document goes on to review other reports regarding fallen containers captured by the Soviets in the area of Ruda. The contents of the seized crates were listed and their fate was further described in great detail. Thus, we know that the Soviets captured nine containers (the tenth fell in the woods and could not be located), of which two crashed on impact, which damaged the weapons within. Yet another container holding food opened spontaneously in the air and its contents became dispersed throughout the area.

The document also describes the preparations preceding the airlift and its course in a surprisingly precise manner. It is likely that the American airmen of Second Lieutenant Johnston's crew, who performed an emergency landing at Brześć (Brest), were quite open and willing to share information with the Soviets.

Our conversation with the crew of the Flying Fortress, which had been damaged by a Focke Wulf 190 and landed at the airfield in Brest, clarified that, on September 18, a group of over 1,000 aircraft [sic], along with 60 Mustang fighters escorting them, was ordered to airlift weapons, ammunition, and food for the insurgents in Warsaw, and then to land in Poltava afterwards.

Before departing, the navigators and pilots were shown aerial photographs of Warsaw and its vicinity. The areas held by the Polish insurgents were marked. In case Warsaw was covered by cloud cover, the containers were to be dropped into the forest to the northwest of Warsaw, which was also controlled by the insurgents. The navigator's map included a marked route to Poltava and the approximate German–Russian front line. The operation was to be conducted at an altitude of 14–20,000 ft.

The navigators of the lead planes had photo drawings (aerial photographs) on their sleeves, which was to ensure sufficient accuracy in dropping the containers.

The air expedition followed a course above the North Sea, Jutland Peninsula, the northern German–Danish border, and the Baltic Sea. In the area east of Kolberg [Kołobrzeg] the planes turned to the southeast toward the area above German territory. Having entered a zone of thick clouds, the planes performed two large circle-like maneuvers while climbing upward, which allowed them to escape the cloud cover and continue on toward Warsaw. The expedition approached Warsaw at an altitude of 17,000 ft. In the area of Modlin, the groups of Flying Fortresses were fired on by anti-aircraft defenses. However, the aircraft in question did not fall into the zone of anti-aircraft fire. It was attacked by one Focke Wulf 190 which suddenly attacked it from the side of the clouds. The Focke-Wulf 190s [sic] were chased by a Mustang, but the gunner feared to open fire lest he damage our plane. The Focke-Wulf 190 damaged the tail of the aircraft. The B-17 became more difficult to steer and the pilot turned toward the Narew [River] and the frontline. The cargo was dropped based on a guesstimate [zgadywanka]. Siedlce and Brest were marked on the map as the closest Soviet airfields. The pilot did not see the airfield in the Siedlce area, so he continued on to Brest, where his landing was a complete success. The flight from England to Brest lasted 8 h. Because the aircraft was damaged, its crew did not observe the airdrops conducted by other planes during the operation.[38]

The document, signed by the Chief-of-Staff of the 16th Soviet Air Army and the chief of its Operational Department, is concluded by an assessment of the Allied airdrops, which were compared with the Soviet ones: "Only the drops conducted by airmen flying our Po-2s [Polikarpov-2s] at night landed over the intended target … we were the only ones to provide real and serious assistance to the Warsaw insurgents."[39] Based on reports generated by the 1st Army of the Polish People's Army, the authors further claimed that "the insurgents were mostly armed with weapons dropped by the planes of the 16th Air Army." Not surprisingly, the Soviet officers did not neglect to also castigate the alleged quarrelsome plotting of the leaders of the Polish reaction, the Home Army figureheads, and the supposedly fascistic inner core of the Home Army's high command.

The memoirs of Sabina Sebyłowa, a resident of Warsaw's eastern Praga district, provide a civilian's perspective on the very same events described by military men.[40] On September 18, the author, along with her son, was viewing the bombers and the escorting fighters, in addition to the parachutes filling the sky. She accurately recognized the aircraft as American. The crazed German anti-aircraft fire also captured her attention. Intrigued by the events, mother and son climbed to the attic of the house at Brzeska Street no. 5 where they resided. From this vantage point they observed parachutes of various colors, pushed by the wind toward the Vistula, through their binoculars. Most likely they were observing the area of the Praga river port from above the roofs of the houses located between them and the river. The river port was located on the opposite side of the Vistula from the Powiśle district, which by then had been abandoned by the insurgents. She recalled: "The Vistula water appeared as if it was boiling. The Germans were firing shells into it to prevent a Polish operation from Praga to reach the airdropped containers." Did some of the containers fall on the right side of the river?

Did the units of the 1st Polish Army attempt to seize them? If so, we do not have information regarding the outcome of such efforts.

★★★

Despite the negative intelligence assessments of the *Frantic* 7 mission over Warsaw, Polish authorities felt they had little choice but to continue pressing for further airdrop efforts. The fate of Poland's future as a free nation hinged on the desperate situation of beleaguered Warsaw. On September 20 and 21, the Council of National Unity in Warsaw sent a thank you letter for the assistance provided to Warsaw to President Roosevelt and Prime Minister Churchill via Polish Prime Minister Mikołajczyk. In the same dispatch the Council also appealed for further airlifts of food and arms for the insurgents. Simultaneously, similar words of gratitude were addressed to Allied commanders responsible for the logistical preparations: the minister of the RAF, Sinclair; the commander of the U.S. Strategic Air Force in Europe, Lieutenant General Spaatz; and the commanders of 8th and 15th Air Armies. The U.S. ambassador in London, John G. Winant, was also thanked.

In spite of the tragic situation in Warsaw, the Poles still hoped for further airlifts for the dying rising. Thus, on September 19, Mikołajczyk sent a request to repeat the operation of September 18 to President Roosevelt, Minister Sinclair, Lieutenant General Spaatz, and British Foreign Secretary Anthony Eden (who played the role of intermediary in these efforts).

On the night of September 24–25, Ambassador Winant, who relayed the views espoused by the Poles, met with Lieutenant General Spaatz and Major General Eaker. In the end, it was decided that further day drops were unfeasible. The main reasons behind the unfavorable decision were that the existing Eastern Command bases in the Soviet Union were to be closed down, the daylight hours were ever shorter, the low assessments of the mission's effectiveness, and the number of lost aircraft or machines left behind in Eastern Command bases.[41]

On September 28, the Council of National Unity directed yet another appeal to Churchill, Stalin, and Roosevelt, informing them that the danger of losing Mokotów district threatened the City Center's ability to resist the Germans further. Thus, immediate assistance in the form of supply airdrops and airstrikes by American aircraft using Soviet bases were absolutely necessary.

The feverish Polish efforts, supported by such appeals and information regarding the critical shortages of food and medical supplies in the city, eventually achieved a partial breakthrough. On September 27, Lieutenant General Spaatz approved plans to carry out another airlift, this time consisting of 72 "Flying Fortresses," 64 Mustangs, and two Mosquitos.[42] Scheduled to depart on September 30, Operation *Frantic 8* required, as always, the consent of the Soviets. Moscow agreed only after being subjected to personal pressure by Winston Churchill himself. Mikołajczyk described the circumstances of the meeting which preceded this approval in his dispatch to the Plenipotentiary of the Polish Government-in-Exile and the Head of the Home Army:

> Today, after exhausting all possibilities to plead with Roosevelt and Churchill via telegram, I personally pleaded with Prime Minister Churchill for help in the form of a great daytime operation. Two hours later, he informed me that the operation will take place as soon as possible. I wish to point out that I was informed of the inclement weather conditions.[43]

Afterwards, the expedition was rescheduled to occur on October 1. Unfortunately, since no signs that the weather would soon improve were forthcoming, the operation was yet again rescheduled to take place on October 2 and then 3. The Poles awaited the expedition with great anticipation and hope, but to no avail. The weather along the air route to Warsaw failed to improve, in spite of expectations.

Meanwhile, on October 2, the Americans were informed by the Soviets that a large number of insurgents were evacuated from Warsaw by the Soviet air force and that only isolated pockets of rebels remained in the city. This claim was false. Thus, Moscow argued, an airlift would only supply the Germans. Citing their own claims, the Soviets refused to consent to any further airlifts, both now and in the future.

Having received such information, the Americans decided to place a hold on Operation *Frantic 8* and requested confirmation from the Poles and the chief of the American Military Mission in Moscow, Major General Deane.

In response, the chief of the U.S. Military Mission explained that the Soviets' negative attitude toward further airlifts was dictated by the fact that over 50% of the previous airdrop fell into German hands. Moreover, he continued, there were no more than 3,000 insurgents fighting in isolated groups in Warsaw at the time. He added that while he did not receive any response from the Soviets regarding their final stance on assistance for Warsaw, he nevertheless predicted that they would not change their position. Simultaneously, the Poles confirmed the information regarding the dramatic situation of the insurgents in Warsaw.

At the time in question, the Polish military authorities in London were aware of General "Bór" Komorowski's dispatch sent to the Chief-of-Staff of the Commander-in-Chief on October 1, which confirmed the decision to lay down arms in the city. As a result, the ceasefire agreement to end fighting in Warsaw was signed on October 2.[44] The uprising was over.

Given the fall of the Polish capital, Mikołajczyk attempted to obtain assistance via airlifts for the remaining Home Army units, located in the areas of Włoszczowa and Proszowice (to the north of Kraków in southern Poland), during the subsequent several days. However, in their consideration of the possible benefits of such a mission, the Americans took into account that the situation of the units concentrated around those localities was not as dramatic as in the case of Warsaw itself. However, these groupings had been supplied by the RAF from its bases in the Mediterranean region, and these supply drops could be continued. The fact that the weather forecasts for the next several days were unfavorable also played a role. The Americans simply did not believe that such large units could survive in the open field behind the front lines. Lastly, they also had to take into account the closing of the Eastern Command bases by October 5.

Taking the above into consideration, the Allies decided to rebuff the Polish pleas and to avoid any delays in liquidating the Eastern Command bases and evacuating their personnel.

On October 4, Lieutenant General Spaatz informed the Eastern Command that *Frantic* would no longer involve supplying Poland. Spaatz also ordered the commander of the EC bases, Major General Walsh, to prepare for winter by continuing to evacuate American personnel and equipment. Since the Soviets had accepted an earlier project to retain a crew of 200 Americans in Poltava, the U.S. hoped that common operations could be renewed in the spring of 1945.[45]

On the following day, Lieutenant General Spaatz's deputy, Major General Anderson, informed the Poles that the Eastern Command bases in the USSR would be closed down and no more American shuttle missions would be flown to Poland.[46]

Meanwhile, on September 28 in Horham, where the command of the 13th Bomber Wing was stationed, the participants of the expedition were awarded Polish medals "in recognition of heroism shown on September 18, 1944 on a flight to bring aid to fighting Warsaw."[47] Colonel Karl Truesdell, Jr., the commander of the 95th Bomber Group, who was in charge of the expedition, was awarded the Polish "Virtuti Militari" Fifth Class silver cross by the Commander-in-Chief, General Sosnkowski, himself. In addition, the Polish Cross of Valor was awarded to airmen in the following units:

390th Bomber Group

Major William J. Jones, commander of the 390th Bomber Group
Captain James M. Miller
Lieutenant Francis E. Akins, the posthumously honored commander of B-17G "I'll Be Seeing You"
Lieutenant James R. O'Neil, the second pilot in the crew of the fallen Lieutenant Hibbard

100th Bomber Group

Second Lieutenant Thomas S. Jeffrey, commander of the 100th Bomber Group

355th Fighter Group:

357th Fighter Squadron:
Major John L. Elder, the leader of the 357th Fighter Squadron
Captain Austin F. Dunlap
354th Fighter Squadron:

Major Bert W. Marshall and Lieutenant Francis Macher, who performed the duties of the commander of the 355th Fighter Group in this expedition 358th Fighter Squadron:

Major Emil L. Sluga, the leader of the 358th Fighter Squadron

The medal ceremony was recounted on October 15, 1944 by *Wings*, the periodical of the Polish Air Force, which quoted the statement of the commander of one of the groups, Lieutenant T. H. Holbrook for the Polish Telegraph Agency: "When we approached Warsaw at about 1 o'clock in the afternoon on September 18, we were fired upon. From our altitude at 12,000 ft we could not see the barricades in the streets, but I'm sure that some of the explosions came from shells exploding between the buildings."[48]

CHAPTER 8

The End of Operation *Frantic* and the Start of the Cold War

The failure of the American resupply effort was not foreordained. Had the drop occurred in August when it was initially planned, nearly all the supplies would have landed in Polish hands and would have constituted significant aid to the Home Army. Given that lack of arms and supplies was perhaps the single biggest problem facing the AK during the Warsaw Uprising, one or more such drops might have changed the military situation on the ground. More significantly, though, it would have indicated to the Soviets a strong Western commitment to the Polish Independentist cause and might even have impelled Soviet ground forces to act more aggressively toward Nazi forces in and around Warsaw.

The political problems of *Frantic 7* were part of the larger issue of relations between the Americans and the Soviets during the war. The *Frantic* operations were conceived in late 1943 as Soviet forces advanced westward into Ukraine, making Soviet airfields accessible to long-range aircraft based in Italy and later in England. *Frantic* reflected the oddly American combination of logistical and technical excellence and political naivety. The idea was to launch shuttle bombing operations in which American aircraft would hit targets in central Europe, such as Hungary, Romania, or occupied Poland, fly to Soviet airbases, refuel and rearm, and then fly back again and bomb additional targets in the same areas. From a military standpoint, this would allow the Allies to hit war industries that the Nazis had moved to the eastern limits of their empire to keep them out of reach of the Allied bombing campaign. Thus no part of the Reich would be immune to air raids.

Nevertheless, the military aspect of *Frantic* was secondary to its political objectives. American political and military leaders foresaw the need to establish closer cooperation with the Red Army as the campaign against Germany reached its final stages, and Allied and Soviet forces drew closer together. Such cooperation was seen as the first step in creating relationships that would continue after the end of hostilities in Europe. America and the USSR, it was believed, would largely direct the affairs of the postwar world in a kind of peaceful condominium. The Americans were eager to establish closer relations, and while Soviet political leadership had vetoed previous initiatives in this direction, the Americans believed they would meet a warmer reception once they were able to initiate direct relations with the Red Army. This stemmed from a mistaken belief that the Soviet Union operated in ways that were roughly analogous to those in the West, albeit somewhat less democratic. Differences and problems with the Soviets were often put down to cultural misunderstandings based on Russia's past and its "understandable" historical experience with foreign invaders.

According to historian Lloyd Gardner:

> The President favored what might be called a two-phased approach to the Soviets. It was his belief that the crucial transition period after the war should be used to build trust among the Big Three. As that trust grew, presumably, the tendency to act unilaterally would fade away of itself. Whatever had to be conceded to reassure Stalin during the war would be redeemed when the transition to a more open world was complete. Admittedly, this was all quite vague in Roosevelt's mind.[1]

The Americans had two additional goals for the *Frantic* plan. First, they hoped that air force cooperation with the Soviets would also lay the groundwork for future operations from Siberia against Japan. (This aspect of the plan was kept from the Soviets.) Second, *Frantic* was planned as a way to show the Soviets that Americans were willing to shoulder their share of the military burden in the struggle against Nazism. Given that the Soviets were facing the largest number of German troops, the Americans wanted to use *Frantic* as a tangible sign of their commitment to the alliance. In American eyes, the *Frantic* plan could perhaps expand beyond strategic bombing so that American planes could be used in an operational capacity in support of Soviet troops.

The Soviets reacted suspiciously to the plans for *Frantic*, assuming that the Americans were primarily interested in gathering intelligence about the Soviet military. (Like the Americans, the Soviets viewed American motives as roughly analogous to their own approach, which saw "cooperation" only as a zero-sum game in which the stronger or more clever side took advantage of the other.) The Soviets responded by raising technical and logistical obstacles to the operation, most of which were specious. Yet American officials pressed the case. This included a personal appeal to Stalin by President Franklin D. Roosevelt and his son Elliott (acting as his father's military advisor) at the Tehran Conference. The Soviets agreed to limited cooperation in shuttle bombing but then dragged their feet for months in responding to American requests and providing needed technical information. By early 1944, the Soviets had the clear upper hand on the Eastern Front and began to see *Frantic* as an easy way to gain information about American military technology. Finally, on June 2, 1944 the first of the seven *Frantic* operations began as an air armada from Italy hit rail marshaling yards in Hungary and subsequently airfields in Romania on June 6 and 11.

A second *Frantic* mission began on June 21. After landing at bases near Poltava, American bombers were subjected to a devastatingly accurate German night raid which caused significant damage to American equipment. Questions persist as to whether the Soviets should have done more to defend the base—its air defenses were clearly inadequate—and why they denied permission for American fighters at Poltava to fly defensive patrols or intercept German reconnaissance aircraft that appeared to be surveying the site the day before. One U.S. author later claimed that the Soviets deliberately let down their guard in order to bring an end to the *Frantic* enterprise and/or to gain aircraft wreckage for intelligence purposes. Following this setback, the *Frantic* missions continued in July though the Soviets appeared increasingly hesitant about the entire program.

It was in this context that the mission to resupply Warsaw appeared, following the outbreak of the Warsaw Uprising on August 1, 1944. Throughout the first half of August, Soviet forces stood idle outside of

Warsaw and Stalin refused permission for the RAF's Polish, British, and Dominion squadrons to land on Soviet airfields after flying from Italy to drop supplies to Warsaw, forcing the crews to conduct dangerous round-trip flights.

At the same time, the Americans sought to use the operational experience and logistical structure created for the *Frantic* operation to drop supplies to the Poles. A three-way debate now developed among the Americans. Washington-based officials, including the White House (thanks in part to the urgings of British Prime Minister Churchill), wanted to push the hardest for Soviet cooperation. U.S. Ambassador to Moscow Averell Harriman was pessimistic about the chances of Soviet approval and lukewarm in his support for the mission. The American air commanders in Europe, perhaps most influenced by contact with their Soviet counterparts, believed that the Soviets might even stop all *Frantic* operations over the Polish dispute and generally opposed using American air assets to help the Poles. The Soviets even canceled a planned American attack on Nazi targets in Koenigsberg (*Frantic 6*), apparently afraid the Americans would use the operation as an excuse to overfly Warsaw with supplies.

While this was going on, the situation of American Army Air personnel based in the Ukraine gradually deteriorated. Soviet security officials restricted the privileges afforded to U.S. servicemen, beginning with contact with female Red Army personnel stationed nearby, and proceeding to the taking of pictures and reducing the general level of food and other comforts (though admittedly these privileges remained above those of their Soviet counterparts). Petty harassment of American personnel became common, including fights and mugging of lone servicemen. Soviet officials accused some Americans of trying to incite anti-Soviet feeling or of making anti-Soviet speeches. (The Soviets made Russian-speaking American personnel a particular target.)

On August 20, Roosevelt and Churchill made a joint appeal to Stalin to approve the airdrop. Again Stalin refused and further Soviet propaganda statements excoriated the Home Army and the insurgents in Warsaw. Similar statements—both public and private—greeted further Allied requests as late as September 5. Nevertheless, the pressure on the Soviets and the potential propaganda fallout of doing nothing to aid Warsaw began to have an effect. Additionally, the Soviets may have believed that the position of the Home Army insurgents could not be saved even with large supply drops. On September 9, the Soviets formally agreed to allow a *Frantic* supply mission to Warsaw. For the next few days, Soviet foot-dragging and weather postponed the mission. It was not until September 17 that the final go-ahead was given and the mission began.

The Soviet effort to use the Warsaw Uprising to destroy pro-independence forces in Poland is well known. Although a few Western and most Russian historians still hew to the line that there was little or nothing the Soviets could have done to aid the Poles, the experience of the *Frantic* operations further highlights Soviet perfidy. The Americans had in place by June 1944 a reasonably successful shuttle bombing operation that hit targets throughout east-central Europe. Although this effort was motivated primarily by political considerations, it was ideal for dropping supplies to the besieged Poles. Moreover, it provided a precedent for other Allied efforts (e.g., British) to get supplies to Warsaw. The Soviets clearly realized this and put a great deal of effort into keeping the *Frantic* operations from being used to help the Home Army. The danger of allowing American air missions to overfly Poland where they might drop supplies to pro-independence Poles caused the Soviets to put a quick end to the whole *Frantic* enterprise which from their perspective had outlived its usefulness.

Yet if part of the goal of *Frantic* had been to provide the basis for future U.S.–Soviet cooperation, it not only failed to do that but contributed to a deepening of suspicion. By the late summer of 1944, the Soviets clearly considered the *Frantic* efforts to be at best an irritant. The official requests to use *Frantic* as a way to supply Warsaw were met with Soviet efforts to end *Frantic* by denying or canceling mission requests, by delaying command-level decisions needed to carry out even the agreed-on shuttle bombing efforts, and by lower-level attempts to make the American presence at Soviet airbases in the Ukraine untenable. While many individual Americans who participated in the *Frantic* operations would remember warmly the assistance of individual Soviet personnel, the overall Soviet attitude created a negative impression and turned a number of U.S. servicemen into dedicated anti-communists.

Norman Davies has suggested that the Warsaw Uprising was the first battle of the Cold War. If he is correct, then surely *Frantic 7* was a major part of the hardening of attitudes that accompanied the start of that conflict. The Americans who experienced the failure of *Frantic* were particularly chagrined by Soviet cynicism toward the fate of Warsaw and its people. Many were middle-ranked career officers whose views would be widely circulated in the American military for years to come. As early as 1945, rumors that Soviet troops had treated the bodies of fallen American fliers in Warsaw disrespectfully were common. American diplomat Arthur Bliss Lane had no qualms laying the deaths of Americans lost in the *Frantic 7* operation at the Soviet's door: "Who knows how many American lives were lost as a result of the brutal policy of liquidating the Polish underground?"[2]

The first six *Frantic* missions had limited military effect on the course of the war. The *Frantic 7* mission to Warsaw could have had a real impact had it occurred earlier in the insurgency when the Poles still controlled a large part of city. The Americans had been able to drop a significant amount of supplies, dwarfing the small but courageous nighttime operations to drop supplies conducted by Polish, British, and South African crews based in Italy. But the seventh *Frantic* mission failed due to Soviet maneuvering and the delays and roadblocks they had imposed on the operation.

At the outset of the *Frantic* operations, American military personnel had fully supported the potential of building cooperation with the Soviets by conducting joint missions and were thus fully in sync with the foreign policy goals of the Roosevelt administration. The events surrounding the Warsaw Uprising and the Soviets' obvious bad faith, however, changed this picture. An increasing sense of unease and distrust that came in the wake of *Frantic 7* was reinforced by further Soviet actions in the years that followed. In the fall of 1944, the disgust expressed by the Army Air Corps officers and personnel toward the Soviet betrayal of the uprising was yet a minority view but it was a seed that would grow quickly in the postwar years.

Orders of Battle, Operation *Frantic* 7, September 1944

German and Hungarian

Luftwaffe: 6th Air Fleet, Warsaw Area

12th Anti-Aircraft Artillery Division, 77th Anti-Aircraft Artillery Regiment

Squadron	Batteries	Location	Main armament
661st	1st and 2nd	Modlin, railway station	Unknown
661st	3rd and 4th	Modlin, Korona Utracka	Five Flak 88 mm guns
22nd Motorized	1st and 3rd	Nowy Dwór	

23rd Anti-Aircraft Artillery Division, 80th Anti-Aircraft Artillery Regiment

Squadron	Batteries	Location	Main armament
296th	1st	Dziekanów Polski	Five Flak 88 mm guns
296th	3rd	Dąbrowa	Six Flak 88 mm guns
296th	4th	Wawrzyszew Nowy	Three Flak 88 mm guns
50th Motorized	1st	Kępa Kiełpińska	Four Flak 88 mm guns
50th Motorized	2nd	Rajszew	Four Flak 88 mm guns
50th Motorized	3rd	Kępa Kiełpińska	Four Flak 88 mm guns

Air Squadrons

Regiment	Squadron	Location	Aircraft
51st Fighter "Mölders"	1st	Kroczewo	Me 109G
51st Fighter "Mölders"	4th	Modlin	Me 109G
10th Attack		Kroczewo	Fw 190 F/G
1st Attack		Modlin	Ju 87 Stuka
4th Bomber	Staff	Nasielsk (Chrcynno)	He 111
54th Fighter "Grünherz"	4th	Nasielsk (Chrcynno)	Fw 190A

Armored and Cavalry Forces

Division	Regiment	Location
19th Niedersachsiche (Lower Saxon) Panzer	27th Panzer	Dziekanów Niemiecki
3rd SS Panzer "Totenkopf" (Death's Head)	Staff of the 6th SS Panzer Grenadier "Theodor Eicke"	Dziekanów Polski
1 Honvéd Lovas Hadosztály (1st Hungarian Cavalry Division)		Łomianki-Dąbrowa

Allied

1. U.S. Army Air Corps, 8th Air Force

Bomber Command

Bomber Group	Commander	Base	Squadrons	Number of aircraft
95th	Col. Karl Truesdell Jr.★	No. 119, Horham, Suffolk	334, 335, 336, and 412	36 B-17s
100th	Lt. Col. Thomas S. Jeffrey	No. 174, Thorpe Abbotts, Suffolk	349, 350, 351, and 418	38 B-17s
390th	Maj. William J. Jones	No. 153, Framlingham (Parham), Suffolk	568, 569, 570, and 571	36 B-17s

Escort Fighters

Fighter Group	Commander	Base	Squadrons	Number of aircraft
361st	Capt. John D. Duncan	No. 374, Bottisham, Cambridgeshire	374, 375, and 376	43 P-51s
4th	Lt. David W. Howe	No. 356, Debden, Cambridgeshire	334, 335, and 336	39 P-51s
355th	Col. Everett W. Stewart	No. 122, Steeple Morden, Cambridgeshire	354, 357, and 358	64 P-51s

★Truesdell was the overall commander of the expedition

2. Polish Home Army

Kampinos Forest Group, from August 8, 1944

Main Unit	Sub-groups	Commander
		Lt. Adolf Pilch "Góra"
Palmiry-Młociny Regiment	I Nalibocki Battalion	Lt. Witold Lenczewski "Strzała"
	II Kampinos Battalion	Capt. Stanisław Nowosad "Dulka"
	27th Ulan Regiment	Lt. Zygmunt Koc "Dąbrowa"
Sochaczew Battalion		Maj. Władysław Starzyk "Korwin"
Legionowo Battalion		Lt. Bolesław Szymkiewicz "Znicz"
Company Lotnicza		Lt. Tadeusz Gaworski "Lawa"
Insurgent Company "Jerzy"		Lt. Jerzy Strzałkowski "Jerzy"
Battalion "Piesc" 1st Company		Lt. Stefan Matuszczyk "Porawa"
Platoon		2nd Lt. Tadeusz Nowicki "Orlik"
Company		2nd Lt. Franciszek Wiszniowski "Jurka"
Half-battalion		2nd Lt. Marian Olszewski "Marysia"
Platoon		2nd Lt. Jerzy Dudziec "Puchały"
Sapper platoon		2nd Lt. Bolesław Janulis "Jurewicz"
Platoon		Lt. Henryk Małowidzki "Rana"

Timeline of Commemorations for the Crew of "I'll Be Seeing You"

August 1980. Strikes by Solidarity Free Trade Union movement begin a period of relative liberalization. Previously forbidden historical topics can be discussed more openly.

May 1981. The establishment of a volunteer group consisting of: Janina and Zygmunt Bogucki, Klemens Bogurat, Marian Drozdowski, Józef Krzyczkowski ("Szymon"), Józef Matuszewski, Andrzej Misiurewicz, Janina and Stanisław Niegodzisz, Maciej Piekarski, Jerzy Sienkiewicz, and Ryszard Szcześniak. The group addressed a letter to Poland's Council of Ministers requesting permission to commemorate the events of September 18, 1944 by unveiling a memorial plate on the wall of the Maria Konopnicka Elementary School in Dziekanów Leśny and renaming a section of Maria Konopnicka Street (the site of the initial grave of the plane's crew) to "The Crew of 'I'll Be Seeing You' Street."

November 16, 1981. The Civic Committee for the Preservation of Monuments to Struggle and Martyrdom agrees to the installation of a memorial plaque.

December 13, 1981–1920 July 1983. Martial law in Poland. Historical censorship reimposed.

September 1984. The formation of the Committee to Commemorate Shot-Down Allied Aircraft Carrying Aid to Insurrectionary Warsaw. The committee consisted of the members of the initial group as well as the local chapter of ZBoWiD [the official veterans' organization in "People's" Poland controlled and licensed by the communist regime] in Łomianki headed by Stanisław Baran, which was to finance the undertaking. After receiving the necessary permission and completing the preparations, the committee planned to unveil the memorial plaque on the elementary school in Dziekanów Leśny. On the day before the planned ceremony the dailies *Życie Warszawy* and *Express Wieczorny* announced its place, date, and time (September 18, 1944, at 1700 h).[1] Alas, the Provincial Committee of the Polish United Workers' Party (i.e., the Communist Party) banned the local chapter of ZBoWiD and the Parish (*Gmina*) Administration from holding the commemoration.

September 18, 1984. *Życie Warszawy* noted that the "Ceremony in Łomianki Deferred. The Board of the ZBoWiD Chapter in Łomianki has reported that the commemoration of the shooting-down of an Allied plane in Dziekanów Leśny during the 40th anniversary of the Warsaw Uprising has been deferred for technical reasons. We will announce the new date of the unveiling."[2]

September 21, 1986. The unveiling of a monument to the crew of "I'll Be Seeing You" at the local cemetery in Kiełpin, which included the plaque which had been prepared for the commemoration in September 1984. The monument was erected through the efforts of the veterans from the local chapter of ZBoWiD in Łomianki.

July 17, 1987. In response to a request to rename one of the streets in Dziekanów Leśny as "United States Airmen Street," the Unit for Naming Residential Complexes, Squares, and Streets in Warsaw, subordinate to a commission of the National Council of the Capital City of Warsaw, replied that "the permission has been granted to rename one of the streets in Dziekanów Leśny, under the condition, however, that the street be renamed after "*Allied Airmen*" [emphasis in original], and not, as specified in the request, "United States Airmen."[3]

September 27, 1987. The Vice President of the United States, George H. W. Bush, and the last living member of the crew of "I'll Be Seeing You," radio operator Marcus L. Shook, visit the cemetery in Kiełpin. Shook was awarded the Warsaw Insurgent Cross.

June 29, 1988. Poland's Council of State posthumously awarded the Warsaw Insurgent Cross to all the remaining crew members of "I'll

Be Seeing You," but for unknown reasons the ground mechanic and side gunner, Platoon Leader Christy, was omitted.

June 1989. Communist party loses partially free parliamentary elections, marking the formal end of communist rule and the origin of the Third Polish Republic.

September 17, 1989. The families of the fallen airmen visit the cemetery in Kiełpin. The ceremony at the cemetery was attended by: Lieutenant Francis E. Akins' wife, Garnett L. Akins Rainey, along with their daughter, Marcia E. Akins Evancheck; Sergeant Paul F. Haney's brother, Arthur Haney, along with his wife, Naomi Haney, and daughters, Suzanne L. Haney, Gery, and June Pollard Haney; Sergeant Walter P. Shimshock's brothers, Bernard Szymczak and George Shimshock and George's wife, Helen Shimshock.

December 1989. The decision to rename one of the streets in Dziekanów Leśny "Allied Airmen" Street is implemented.

February 1990. Shook's second visit in Łomianki and Kiełpin. A statuette of "I'll Be Seeing You," created by Joe Adams of Oregon, is brought to Poland.

March 6, 1990. The statuette of "I'll Be Seeing You" is presented, on Shook's behalf, to the Historical Museum of the Capital City of Warsaw by the Air Attaché of the U.S. Embassy, Col. Thomas E. Snodgrass.

May 1990. The School Committee to Commemorate the Crew of the American Plane "I'll Be Seeing You" is established at the Maria Konopnicka Elementary School in Dziekanów Leśny.

July 13, 1991. A Sister City agreement is signed between Łomianki (Poland) and Columbia Heights (Minnesota). A moving force behind this initiative is Columbia Heights resident Bernard Szymczak, brother of Sergeant Shimshock.

September 18, 1991. A memorial plaque is installed and unveiled on the wall of the Maria Konopnicka Elementary School.

1992. The Columbia Heights–Łomianki Sister Cities Social Committee is established.

October 1992. Lipowa Street in Dziekanów Leśny is renamed after Francis Akins, the commander of the bomber.

February 24, 1994. Shook is awarded honorary citizenship of Łomianki.

August 2, 1994. U.S. Vice President Al Gore visits Kiełpin Cemetery.

January 22, 1995. The death of the last crew member of "I'll Be Seeing You," Marcus L. Shook.

May 1996. A street in Dziekanów Leśny is renamed in honor of "Sergeant Władysław Szymczak" [Walter Shimshock], the bomber's tail gunner.

Endnotes

Preface

1 Anne Applebaum, *Iron Curtain: The Crushing of Eastern Europe, 1944–1956* (New York: Doubleday, 2012). See, by comparison, Frank Costigliola, *Roosevelt's Lost Alliances: How Personal Politics Helped Start the Cold War* (Princeton: Princeton University Press, 2010). The epitome of Cold War relativism was perhaps the CNN documentary miniseries *Cold War*, which aired in 24 episodes in 1998.

Chapter 1

1 Dispatch dated July 7, 1944 to the Head Commander of the Home Army, Gen. Tadeusz "Bór" Komorowski.

2 Norman Davies, *Rising '44: The Battle for Warsaw* (New York: Viking, 2003), 609–610.

3 Ibid., 249.

4 Andrzej Dryszel, *"Masakara Woli," Tygodnik Przegląd: Archiwum no. 31* (2011); Włodzimierz Nowak and Angelika Kuźniak, „Mój warszawski szał," *Gazeta Wyborcza*, August 23, 2004 (English translation at www.warsawuprising.com).

5 Central Commission for Investigation of German Crimes in Poland, *German Crimes in Poland* (New York: Howard Fertig, 1982), record 63. Polish witnesses often used the term "Ukrainians" or "Vlasov's men" for the Germans' ex-Soviet auxiliaries. Ukrainian formations serving under German command were not present during most of the uprising although some Ukrainians did serve in SS-Sturmbrigade RONA. The RONA brigade was so brutal and ineffective it was withdrawn from fighting by the Germans and assigned to guard a sector of the Kampinos Forest outside the city. On the night of September 2–3, a detachment of the Home Army's Kampinos Forest command wiped out two battalions of RONA troops in the villages of Truskaw and Marianów.

6 Nowak and Kuźniak, „Mój warszawski szał."
7 Ibid.
8 Julian Eugene Kulski, *Dying We Live: The Personal Chronicle of a Young Freedom Fighter in Warsaw, 1939–1945* (New York: Holt, Rinehart and Winston, 1979).
9 Teresa Wilska 'Bozenka,' Zoska Battalion. *Diary*. Courtesy of the Polish Academic Information Center at the State University of New York at Buffalo. http://www.warsawuprising.com/witness/wilska1.htm

Chapter 2

1 Balkan Allied Air Force, commanded by Air Vice Marshal William Elliot. The grouping included: 334th RAF Special Task Wing, 1586th Squadron, 148 RAF Special Task Squadron, 624th RAF Special Task Squadron, 62nd USAAF Air Transport Group, and 36 aircraft of the Italian Air Force.
2 The SOE was founded in July 1940 to deal with intelligence work, diversionary activities, and sabotage in Axis-occupied countries. The SOE's Polish Section was established to cooperate with Department VI of the (Polish) Staff of the Commander-in-Chief (Cooperation with the Homeland).
3 The 1st Independent Airborne Brigade (*Samodzielna Brygada Spadochronowa*) was led by Gen. Stanisław Sosabowski. As a result of handing the brigade over to the disposal of the British (March 1944), the unit was incorporated into the 1st Allied Airborne Army. On September 18–26, 1944 the brigade fought in Holland, cooperating with the 1st British Airborne Assault Division in the Arnhem–Driel area (Operation *Market Garden*). As a result, the brigade lost 378 killed, wounded, and/or missing men.
4 Contrary to prior British declarations, flights to Poland had been significantly curtailed due to "technical reasons." The real cause of this state of affairs was the fact that Poland had been relegated to the Soviet sphere of influence. Thus, the British feared arming forces unsympathetic to Moscow.
5 Testimony from 1973 in Janusz Kazimierz Zawodny, *Uczestnicy i świadkowie powstania warszawskiego. Wywiady* [The Participants and Witnesses of the Warsaw Uprising: Interviews] (Warsaw: IPN, 2004), 352.
6 Yet he was not alone in his views at the time. The Allied commander in the Mediterranean region, Gen. Henry M. Wilson, and the RAF's Chief-of-Staff, Marshal Charles Portal, largely shared his views on the issue of airdrops into Poland.
7 John Slessor, *The Central Blue. Recollections and Reflections* (London: Cassell and Comp. Ltd., 1956), 612.
8 Poland's President Raczkiewicz intervened twice with Prime Minister Churchill.
9 Dispatch dated July 4, 1944 in *Armia Krajowa w dokumentach 1939–1945. Lipiec–październik 1944, Studium Polski Podziemnej: Londyn* [The Home Army in Documents, 1939–1945: July–October 1944, a Study of Underground Poland: London], vol. VI (Zakład Narodowy im. Ossolińskich Wydawnictwo: Wrocław, 1991), 53.

10 Winston S. Churchill, *Druga wojna światowa* [The Second World War], vol. 6, book 1 (Gdańsk: Phantom Press, 1996), 138.

11 *Armia Krajowa w dokumentach 1939–1945. Lipiec–październik 1944*, 491.

12 Operation *Dragoon* was an Allied amphibious landing on August 15, 1944 in southern France. The objective was to relieve Allied forces fighting in northern France in the wake of the Normandy landings. Operation *Dragoon* helped clear the Germans out of France.

13 Winston S. Churchill, *Druga wojna światowa* [The Second World War], vol. 6, book 1 (Gdańsk: Phantom Press, 1996), 139.

14 Jan M. Ciechanowski, *Na tropach tragedii. Powstanie warszawskie 1944* [The Origins of a Tragedy: The Warsaw Uprising, 1944] (Warsaw: Polska Oficyna Wydawnicza „BGW", 1992), 335–337.

15 *Polskie siły zbrojne w drugiej wojnie światowej* [The Polish Military During the Second World War], vol. III, *Armia Krajowa* [the Home Army] (London: Instytut Historyczny im. Gen. Sikorskiego, 1950), 798.

Chapter 3

1 *Dziennik Polski i Dziennik Żołnierza* [The Polish Daily and the Soldier's Daily], no. 226, September 23, 1944.

2 The difference between the various times provided in this book stems from the fact that some testimonies have utilized both British time (according to most American reports: 1200 h.) and local time (Polish and German testimonies, in spite of the 1-h difference between them, local German [1300 h.] and Polish [1400 h.] time during this period both listed 1300 h.) and, later on, also Soviet time (1500 h. in Soviet testimonies).

3 *Dziennik Polski i Dziennik Żołnierza*, no. 226, September 23, 1944.

4 A Pathfinder/Pathfinder Force (PFF) referred to a bomber equipped with an H2X radar disguised under the name of "Mickey." It was the lead bomber, guiding bombers belonging to other divisions or groups toward the objective. The Pathfinder's initiation of the airdrop was a signal for the remaining planes to drop their cargos.

5 Based on data in: Józef Garliński, *Politycy i żołnierze* [Politicians and Soldiers] (London: n.p., 1971), 207, and Janusz Kazimierz Zawodny, *Nothing but Honour. The Story of the Warsaw Uprising 1944* (Stanford, CA: Hoover Institution Press, 1978), 133 (published in Polish as: *Powstanie warszawskie w walce i dyplomacji* [Warsaw: Wydawnictwo Naukowe PWN, 1994], 180). In some cases the units of measurement were given, while in others they were not. According to credible information, the containers were filled by the American logistical base "Zone H," which worked for the OSS. The base, which functioned as of January 1944, was located near the English village of Holme in Derbyshire. For more on the base itself see: Jerzy Szcześniak, "Operation Carpetbagger," *Lotnictwo*, nos. 1 and 2, 2009.

6 Data based on: *Microfilm A 5689: USSAFE, Warsaw Dropping Operation*. In some cases the units of measurement were given, but not in others.

7 K ration/Field Ration Type K: 3,000-calorie kits prepared for use in battlefield situations in which access to other types of food was impossible. A typical dinner pack contained: a can of a cheese product, two types of tea biscuits, sweetened milk, a synthetic lemon powder for preparing beverages, sugar tablets, four cigarettes, chewing gum, and an additional packet of type-D rations intended for slower consumption with the option of dissolving the mix in boiling water. Ingredients: chocolate, sugar, powdered milk, cocoa fat, oat flower, vitamins, and artificial flavors. Individual products were packed in impermeable packaging consisting of cellophane and waxed cardboard. The entirety was labeled accordingly.

8 Most likely the Polish Section of the SOE. Others sources (Józef Garliński, *Politycy i żołnierze*, and Kajetan Bieniecki, *Lotnicze wsparcie Armii Krajowej* [Air Support for the Home Army]) suggest that the entire cargo was prepared (not without certain logistical problems) by SOE's Polish Section.

9 In early 1944 the formation used was once again changed. Unlike previously, the goal of this change was not to increase the defensive strength of the formation but to ensure better cooperation with the accompanying fighters by reducing the area under observation. The new formation consisted of three divisions of 12 aircraft each. Each formed the shape of the letter "V" and the aircraft flew in a cascading formation. A 36-aircraft bomber group measured 476 m in width, 247 m in length, and 183 m in depth. Individual bomber groups flew at the same altitude, one after another, with 6.4 km gaps in between.

10 Zero Hour (ZH): 0730, objective: ZH + 303 min. (1203), bases: ZH + 535 min. (1555).

11 It belonged to the 3rd Division, 325th Photographic Reconnaissance Wing, 25th Bomber Group, which consisted of Squadrons 652, 653, and 654, stationed at base no. 376, Watton, Norfolk.

12 The Poles used an "iodoform" to convey messages to occupied Poland using broadcasts of the BBC's Polish Radio with a certain set of melodies. Thus, "Jeszcze jeden Mazur" ("One More Mazur") meant the beginning of the operation, while "Marsz Piechoty" ("The March of the Infantry") signified its cancellation. See: Kazimierz Malinowski, *Żołnierze łączności walczącej Warszawy* [The Communications Soldiers in Fighting Warsaw] (Warsaw: Instytut Wydawniczy PAX, 1983), 271–75.

13 Middle European (Time) Zone.

14 *Armia Krajowa w dokumentach 1939–1945. Lipiec–październik 1944, Studium Polski Podziemnej: Londyn* [The Home Army in Documents, 1939–1945: July–October 1944, a Study of Underground Poland: London], vol. IV (Zakład Narodowy im. Ossolińskich, Wydawnictwo: Wrocław, 1991), 346.

15 Control Point: a point designated along the flight path.

16 Flak/*Flugabwehrkanone* (German): anti-aircraft artillery.

17 Damages: four P-51s damaged by enemy aircraft and one by Flak fire, one plane was MIA (Sec. Lt. Arrants). Wins scored: 374th Fighter Squadron, one plane destroyed in the air (Lt. Madison L. Bryant), one plane destroyed on the ground/one plane destroyed on the ground (Lt. Alfred B. Cook), one plane destroyed on the ground/four destroyed on the ground (Lt. Alfred B. Maclay), one plane damaged on the ground (Lt. Thomas J. Moore); 375th Fighter Squadron: one He 111 shot down in the air (Lt. Urban L. Drew), one BV 222 destroyed on the ground (jointly Lt. William D. Rogers and Lt. Lee C. Travis); 376th Fighter Squadron, one plane shot down in the air (Lt. Will T. Butts and Lt. Claude W. Hanley), one plane destroyed in the air (Lt. John B. Bricker).

18 The Mustangs of the 4th Fighter Group took off at 0720 h and returned to base at 1415 h. After completing their mission and upon their return to Britain, around 1300–1330 h, in the area of Lake Muritz, the group noticed a German Me 262 machine approaching from the rear of the 336th Squadron at an altitude of 19,000 ft. Hence, the squadron decided to turn around and pursued the enemy for about 12 min. At the time the German plane did not change its altitude and maintained a certain distance and a position suitable for attacking. The pilot of one P-51 accelerated but was unable to approach the enemy. Of all the Mustangs belonging to the 4th and 361st Fighter Groups a total of nine turned around for various reasons.

19 Miastko in Poland's Western Pomerania.

20 The planes of the 355th Fighter Group took off at 0813 h. In total, 72 Mustangs departed. Eight of them (including the reserve machines) turned around to return. Of the 358th Fighter Squadron four pilots returned and landed in Britain: Lt. Blaylock at 1000 h (damaged radio); and reserve pilots, Lieutenants Roberts, Brown, and Masters, at 1135 h.

21 The Special Squadron codenamed "Borax" consisted of pilots from three squadrons of the 355th Fighter Group as well as the 4th and 361st Groups.

22 Maj. John L. Elder was one of the 355th Fighter Group's most effective pilots (fourth place, eight kills) and piloted a Mustang P-51 B, serial no. 42-106732.

23 The 390th Bomber Group consisted of 36 in three divisions: Division A in the front, C in the rear, and B above both. Each division consisted of 12 aircraft grouped in four three-plane formations. The divisions were commanded by: A: Maj. William J. Jones; B: Maj. Bernard Campbell, divisional codename "Fireball Green"; C: Capt. Robert D. Brown.

24 Jerzy Shiller, "Dziesięciu z Latającej Fortecy" [Ten Airmen from a Flying Fortress] in *Lotnictwo, Aviation International*, no. 14 (July 16–31, 1994), 32. The author was unable to verify the original source of the quote.

25 Maciej J. Kwiatkowski, „ *Tu mówi powstańcza Warszawa*"...: *Dni powstania w audycjach Polskiego radia i dokumentach niemieckich* ["Insurrectionary Warsaw Here" ...: The Warsaw Uprising in the Programming of the Polish Radio and German Documents] (Warsaw: 1994), 488.

26 Shiller, "Dziesięciu z Latającej Fortecy," 32. The author was unable to verify the original source of the quote.

27 An Initial Point marking the beginning of the bombing path is usually located approximately 20 miles away from the target. Individual divisions constituting a bomber group performed turns with delays of a dozen or so seconds upon reaching this point to avoid a jam around the target. Thus, they approached the objective at different angles. Sometimes various divisions were also assigned separate IPs. Usually the flight along the path lasted 7–10 min.

28 Tracking fire was constant firing against a moving object being tracked by a radar or optical means. Maneuvers were conducted to avoid enemy anti-aircraft fire or fighters, based on altering the flight direction and altitude. This was also known as "zig-zagging."

29 Division C turned 6 miles before its designated IP between Cieksyn and Nasielsk.

30 *3rd Bomb Division Mission Reports*, microfilm B 5482. The cited document lists the IP's coordinates as 52 40 N 20 40 E, a location to the east of Nowe Miasto in Poland's Mazovia Province.

31 Ibid.

32 Ibid. RP (Rally Point): a rendezvous point following the completion of the assignment. In the case of the operation in question, these points were located in the area of: Radzymin–Mińsk Mazowiecki (95th Bomber Group, Division C: 52 23 N, 21 36 E, 100th Bomber Group, Division A: 52 21 N, 21 36 E).

33 Ibid. The bomb release line was a line designated around an attacked area or facility above which the aircraft should release its bombs to hit the target.

34 Ibid.

35 Ibid.

36 The number of enemy aircraft given in American testimonies varies greatly. The number provided here is contained in American reports in the collection *355th Fighter Group*, microfilm B 0313.

37 Lt. Henry W. Brown "Babby" was the *355th Fighter Group's* most effective pilot (14.20 wins in the air, 14.50 on the ground) and flew a Mustang P-51 D-5-NA, serial no. 44-13305, code no. WR ★ Z, "The Hun Hunter/Texas." On October 3, after his aircraft was damaged by Flak, he was taken prisoner.

38 Victories: 354th Fighter Squadron—one plane destroyed in the air/one plane damaged in the air/one plane damaged on the ground—Capt. Henry W. Brown/357th Fighter Squadron—one plane destroyed in the air—Maj. Jack [John] L. Elder/one plane destroyed in the air—Capt. Henry H. Kirby Jr./358th Fighter Squadron—one plane destroyed in the air/one plane destroyed in the air—Lt. Ralph Michelena.

39 The target of a head-on attack is the bomber's cockpit. The tactic was pioneered by Polish air force fighter pilots during the September campaign of 1939 and was ultimately used by all air forces, and by 1944 had evolved significantly from its first application. The high speed of the attacker approaching his target shortened the time during which he was under enemy fire to a few seconds. Initially, the planes

approached the attacked formation from the rear. During this time, the enemy formation's course, altitude, and speed were determined, after which it was circumvented on one of its sides. About 3 km in front of the lead bombers the fighters performed a 180° turn, after which the machines adjusted their flight path and initiated the attack. Each pilot attacked a previously selected victim. After the attack, he flew right above or below the bomber while attempting to dodge enemy fire.

40 In his testimony, the commander of the 355th Fighter Group, Maj. Marshall, stated that this decision was dictated by fuel conservation considerations. Before the expedition, each pilot was instructed to save fuel by remaining close to the escorted bombers and to avoid long-distance pursuits of potential Luftwaffe aircraft. Because German fighters had been quite passive for the past several months, the command was very difficult to obey, for the young pilots were eager to fight. In this situation, the Germans considered themselves "lucky" when the Americans broke off pursuit, while the U.S. airmen were happy to note the insignificant level of German activity in the air.

41 The fragment cited here was originally contained in Viktor Kittel's 2009 letter to the member of the Tradytor Association, Wojciech Wieteska, which was made available to the author by Marcin Biegas. The American aircraft of the Thunderbolt and Lightning type did not take part in the expedition. The alleged participation and deaths of platoon leaders Bruno Behrke and Georg Zeilder from Jadgeschwader 54 "Grűnherz" is also uncertain and the author has been unable to corroborate it.

42 Peters flew a Mustang P-51 D-5-NA, serial no. 44-13675, code no. YF ✶ X; Vigna piloted a Mustang P-51 C-1-NT, serial no. 42-103317, code no. YF ✶ M.

43 Based on Szabłowski's account presented in the author's presence in 2001 and 2003. The German units were most likely the elements of the 3rd Panzer Division.

44 The plane fell in a square between the villages of Kątne, Wymysły, Konary, and Winniki in Mazovia.

45 Testimony provided to author in 2003.

46 Known as Dulag Luft, and located 13 km to the northwest of Frankfurt-am-Mein, Auswertestelle West was the largest facility for interrogating captured Allied airmen. Before being assigned to a permanent POW camp, most of the captured airmen were first delivered here.

47 According to the American translation of the document, the location in question is 52 26 N–20 40 E, i.e., the area of Modlin Fortress, which does not correspond to the actual crash site.

48 *Individual Deceased Personnel File–Joseph J. Vigna.*

49 *Individual Deceased Personnel File–Joseph J. Vigna.* Another contemporary mention, consisting of a few sentences, supplements the above testimony by adding that no parachutes were seen during the fight.

50 According to unspecified German sources researched by Maj. Marshall after the war, they reported the shooting down of only one American plane. See Maj.

Marshall's report: "September 18–account." The information provided by Bill Marshall states that the pilot of the other Mustang could have been Lt. Robert M. Thompson.

51 Postwar American documents indicate that the pilot's remains were not burned.

52 Reports provide different numbers of aircraft, 20, 30, 40, or even 50–60, as well as different directions of attack. According to the submitted reports, the zeal of the attackers was so great that the German pilots completely disregarded the fire of their own anti-aircraft artillery. Thus, red flares fired by the Flak guns, most likely warning rounds, were noticed.

53 Roller coaster: The starting position for such an attack was high above the target. Employing a rapid and shallow dive, the attacker passed by the escorting fighters and reached a point 1.5 km behind the bombers and 500 m below them. At this point, to reduce speed, the pilot pulled the nose of the plane up, conducted a conventional attack, and withdrew downward. A sneak attack was used to attack bombers both from the rear and the front of the formation. An attack was launched from the level of the formation or from below, using the clouds or the sun to one's advantage. The height of the attack depended on the position vis-à-vis the target. An attack from below and from the rear was aimed against bombers no. 5, 6, or sometimes 4. After completing the attack (about 300 m from the target) the assailant, who had attacked from a 7 o'clock direction, withdrew by ascending by turning to the left and upward. A frontal attack from below was aimed at the planes leading the formation. Thus, bombers no. 1 and 2 were most often attacked from 1 o'clock. After completing the attack (400 m from the target), the fighter withdrew by first turning leftward and then cutting across the line of his flight by moving to the rear and upward.

54 Conversino, *Fighting with the Soviets: The Failure of Operation FRANTIC 1944–1945* (Lawrence: University Press of Kansas, 1997), 151.

55 The crew of "Bugs Bunny" had constituted a team since its formation in the United States. The flight of September 18, 1944 was its 27th mission. The crew left the Soviet Union for Italy via the Middle East in October 1944. Once in Italy, the crew members were seen by doctors who decided to send them home to the U.S. prior to their completion of the required tour of duty, normally consisting of 35 missions. The doctors determined that the airmen had sustained wounds and were, generally, in poor condition due to their experiences and the loss of their pilot.

56 The number of enemy planes shot down differs from one report to another. Those claiming to have shot down enemy planes were: V. J. Stefanek, one Bf 109 (ultimately, Stefanek was credited with destroying half of an Me 109 on 18 September); A. K. Rogers, one Bf 109; R. C. Foppiano, one Bf 109; G. R. Waite, one Bf 109; C. A. Hoffman, one Bf 109; W. L. Fletcher and J. R. McCaw, one Fw 190; G. W. Popelka, one Bf 109.

57 Platoon Leader Vincent J. Stefanek ("Vin," "Vinny," "Vince"), was born on September 23, 1924 in Cleveland, Ohio and died on November 30, 2010. His roots reached back to his mother's town of Nemsova in Slovakia. He was a member of Lt. Akins' training crew. After the crew arrived in Britain, Stefanek was transferred to a group of reserve gunners. He participated in five more missions before the end of the war. His report was initially given to an intelligence officer on September 23, 1944.

58 Of all the machines in the 390th Bomber Group this one boasted the greatest number of missions: 114. Thus, in an aviation world given to superstition and shaped by the reality of combat, it must have been viewed a particularly lucky machine.

59 Translation of author's original correspondence with Vincent J. Stefanek from 2004.

Chapter 4

1 Władysław Szpilman, *Pianista* [The Pianist] (Kraków: Wydawnictwo ZNAK, 2003), 156.

2 Zygmunt Zaremba, *Wojna i konspiracja* [War and the Underground] (London: B. Świderski, 1957), 262.

3 Tadeusz Komorowski, *Armia Podziemna* [The Underground Army] (London: SPP, 1979), 330–331.

4 Zbigniew Brym-Zdunin, *Żelazna Reduta: Kompania Zdunina w Powstaniu Warszawskim zgr. „Chrobry II"* [The Iron Redoubt: Zdunin's Company in the Warsaw Uprising, the "Chrobry II" Grouping] (London: Polska Fundacja Kulturalna, 1992), 217–218.

5 Wacław Zagórski (Lech Grzybowski), *Wicher wolności, Dziennik powstańca* [The Wind of Freedom: The Diary of an Insurgent] (Warsaw: Czytelnik, 1990), 221–222.

6 The area of the Iron Gate Square (*Plac Żelaznej Bramy*).

7 Puławska Street no. 113 a.

8 Lesław M. Bartelski, *Mokotów, Warszawskie Termopile 1944* [Mokotów: Warsaw's Thermopylae, 1944] (Warsaw: Fundacja Warszawa walczy 1939–1945, 2004), 115.

9 *Armia Krajowa w dokumentach 1939–1945. Lipiec–październik 1944, Studium Polski Podziemnej: Londyn* [The Home Army in Documents, 1939–1945: July–October 1944, a Study of Underground Poland: London], vol. VI (Zakład Narodowy im. Ossolińskich Wydawnictwo: Wrocław, 1991), 347.

10 Alexandrian Microfiche: *Kriegstagebuch Nr. 11 der Führungsabteilung Textband (1. Ausfertigung) Berichtszwit 11.07.44 – 31.12.44. AOK 9.*

11 Maciej J. Kwiatkowski, *"Tu mówi powstańcza Warszawa": Dni powstania w audycjach Polskiego Radia i dokumentach niemieckich* [This is Insurgent Warsaw Speaking:

The Days of the Uprising in the Programming of the Polish Radio and German Documents] (Warsaw: Państwowy Instytut Wydawniczny, 1994), 489.

12 However, a report from September 20, 1944 states that "On September 18 in the area of Warsaw, the anti-aircraft artillery shot down three four-engine American and two Russian planes, and the 3rd Panzer Army shot down one Russian plane. Alexandrian Microfiche: *Oberkommando der Heeresgruppe Mitte Tagesmeldung 19.09.1944/20.09.44/1.00 Uhr/I a Nr. T 4864/44 tjn.*

13 Alexandrian Microfiche: *Armeeoberkommando 9/19.09.1944/ 7.20 Uhr/An Oberkomando Heeresgruppe Mitte/I a Nr. T 13036/44 tjn.*

14 Kwiatkowski, "*Tu mówi powstańcza Warszawa*," 497.

15 Norman Davies, *Powstanie' 44* (Krakow: Wydawnictwo ZNAK, 2004), 503–504.

16 *Der Einsatz der Luftflotte 6 im Rahmen des Kampfes um Warschau vom 1.8.–2.10.1944*, RL 7 / 554, Bundesarchiv, Militärarchiv, Freiburg.

Chapter 5

1 The two indicated locations (Babice Stare in Mazovia Province, and the Pelcowizna area in Warsaw, respectively) are not associated with the site where the bomber actually crashed. These sites are marked by the geographic coordinates of 52 15 N, 20 50 E (or, as another report indicates, 52 17 N, 21 00 E).

2 See Gerhard Aders and Werner Held, *Jadgeschwader 51 „Mölders" Eine Chronik Berichte—Erlebnisse—Dokumente* (Stuttgart: Motorbuch Verlag, 1999). Lt. Günther Josten (1921–2004) was, at the time, the commander of the 3rd Squadron of the 1st Division of the 51st Fighter Regiment "Mölders," classified as "Experte" pilot, which roughly corresponded with the Allied term of "ace." He underwent his baptism of fire over Norway in November 1941. During the war, he scored a total of 178 kills (all of them on the Western Front, including one four-engine B-17), and was awarded a Knight's Cross with an Oak Leaf.

3 Lt. Kurt Dombacher, who flew in JG 51, also reported shooting down a B-17 near Warsaw around 1343 h at a height of 3,500 m. The documents available to the author do not mention anything to corroborate that a JG 51 shot down two previously mentioned American fighters in the area of Nasielsk near Warsaw.

4 The fuel tanks located in the wings were attached between the engines and in the spaces dividing the fuselage from the engine itself.

5 According to the procedures in place before the reduction of the numerical strength of the crews, the airmen were to bail out through the main entrance in the right rear section of the aircraft in the following order: 1. Left gunner, Haney; 2. Right gunner, Christy; 3. Bottom turret gunner, Mac Phee. The remaining members of the crew, bombardier Merrill and navigator Berenson, were to bail out through an entry hatch in the left front part of the fuselage. Tail gunner Shimshock was to jump through his own exit in the rear of the fuselage, while the radio operator Shook, pilot Akins, second pilot Shaw, and the top turret gunner De Cillis were to

leap from the emptied bomb chamber. Because the crew was deprived of the right gunner, his place was taken by the radio operator Shook.

6 Marcus L. Shook's written statement contained in his letter to Ryszard Szcześniak. For the sake of continuity, some statements have been omitted without indicating the exact fragments which have been excised. Comments in parentheses are the author's. In the English edition of this book, the Polish translation of the letter has been retranslated into English without having access to the original letter.

7 Testimony shared in the presence of Ryszard Szcześniak.

8 The report of the 3rd Bomber Division states that an earlier drop was conducted by the bombardier in charge of Division C (390th Bomber Group), Lt. Gerald H. Farris, who was convinced that he received such an order. However, in the report of the 100th Bomber Group of Division C, the leading navigator, 2nd Lt. John D. Carpenter, states that a drop was conducted at the point 52 24 N, 20 45 E, in the Czosnów–Cząstków area. The few photographs that survived confirm that the cargo was dropped in an area delineated by the localities of Zakroczym–Modlin–Wymysły (photograph no. 46/47/48/49), and probably also over the temporary German Vistula River crossing at Kępa Kiełpińska (photograph no. 71). The radio-navigation and visual-compass navigation method utilized at the time was imprecise, but this error is difficult to understand, particularly since the area of Modlin provides plenty of quite good natural linear landmarks, such as the Vistula River, and Narew River, which flows into the Vistula from the east, as well as other landmark objects: the extensive area of Modlin Fortress and the adjacent bridges on the Vistula and Narew.

9 Zygmunt Skarbek-Kruszewski, *Bellum Vobiscum War Memoirs*, available online at the website www.skarbek.com.au/bv/.

10 Testimony given in the author's presence in 2001.

11 *Missing Air Crew Report 10205/Individual Casualty Questionnaire/Casualty Questionnaire.*

12 Ibid.

13 A designated crew member communicated with the rest of the crew every 15 min to check on their psychological and physical state. A lack of oxygen above 8,000 m could cause a sudden and unexpected death within minutes.

14 No name is mentioned, but it most likely refers to Platoon Leader James Christy.

15 *Missing Air Crew Report 10205/Individual Casualty Questionaire/Casualty Questionaire.*

16 Mark J. Conversino, *Fighting with the Soviets: The Failure of Operation FRANTIC 1944–1945* (Lawrence: University Press of Kansas, 1997), 150. Channel C is the emergency homing channel, a radio frequency used to communicate in emergency situations.

17 Testimony given in the author's presence in 2004.

18 Ibid.

19 Ibid.

20 Reports contained in this collection on "kills" and the combat itself, which had been created by the various German Flak batteries, offer a great variety of detailed information, including: the weather conditions, the altitude and speed of the American aircraft, the weaponry at the disposal of the anti-aircraft artillery batteries, the number of projectiles fired by them, and, finally, the number of captured and/or killed members of enemy air crews. In addition to such reports, the collection also contains official documents drafted at various times, such as letters summing up the results of the fighting, requests issued by the Luftflotte 6, and the decisions of the Oberkommando der Luftwaffe, in addition to written testimonies associated with these documents and penned by 24 witnesses, NCOs, and officers from units which were at the time stationed in the area delineated by the following localities: Kazuń, Modlin, Rajszew, Dziekanów Polski, Dziekanów Niemiecki, Kępa Kiełpińska, Dąbrowa, and Wawrzyszew.

21 The reports written at this time by JG 51 and the 5th SS-Panzer Division Wiking were not classified as credible or even true by an employee of the Bundesharchiv–Militärarchiv in Freiburg in response to a query.

22 RL 5 *Luftwaffenpersonalamt Abschußanerkenntnisse Flak*, 314, p. 265, Bundesarchiv–Militärarchiv Freiburg.

23 Ibid., p. 273.

24 We cannot rule out that the descending aircraft was "finished off" by the batteries of 50th Squadron once the machine flew between its positions in the area of Dziekanów Polski.

25 RL 5 *Luftwaffenpersonalamt Abschußanerkenntnisse Flak*, 314, p. 248, Bundesarchiv–Militärarchiv Freiburg.

26 Ibid., p. 223.

27 Ibid.

28 RL 5 *Luftwaffenpersonalamt Abschußanerkenntnisse Flak*, 68, p. 9, Bundesarchiv–Militärarchiv Freiburg.

29 RL 5 *Luftwaffenpersonalamt Abschußanerkenntnisse Flak*, 314, p. 242, Bundesarchiv–Militärarchiv Freiburg.

30 Ibid., p. 275.

31 Ibid.

32 The vertical range of 88 mm heavy anti-aircraft guns was 10,600 m, while 20 mm light anti-aircraft guns had a maximum range of 4,800 m.

33 RL 5 *Luftwaffenpersonalamt Abschußanerkenntnisse Flak*, 314, p. 225, Bundesarchiv–Militärarchiv Freiburg.

Chapter 6

1 Approximately 900 m. The descent speed using parachutes during this time was about 1,000 ft/min.

2 Marcus L. Shook's written statement contained in his letter to Ryszard Szcześniak. For the sake of continuity, some statements have been omitted without indicating the exact fragment excised. In the English edition of this book, the Polish translation of the letter has been retranslated into English without having access to the original letter.

3 Currently Rolnicza Street 313.

4 A conversation later conducted by the author with Marcus L. Shook during his visit in Poland allows us to suppose that the airman seen by K. Bogurat, S. Pasternak, and R. Szcześniak was most likely Shook.

5 Currently Rolnicza Street 309.

6 This is the general area currently marked by the following streets: Graniczka-Kolejowa, Asnyka, Miła, and Rodziewiczówny. The wreck came to rest approximately halfway in between Graniczka-Kolejowa and Miła Streets in the vicinity of the local road (currently Asnyka Street) then running from the village to the Warsaw–Modlin road (currently Graniczka Street).

7 The city housed a forced labor camp and a POW camp for privates and NCOs: Stalag XXI Wollstein. It was operational from 1939 to 1943. Not only Poles, but also British and French POWs, were imprisoned there. In 1942–1943, it held exclusively Soviets and a few Poles. There is little specific information on the camp's fate in 1944–1945. It was located in the northeastern part of the town on the premises of the Koronowo Estate (the area of current-day Strzelecka and Kręta Streets). The camp hospital was located in an area adjacent to the neighboring property known as "Strzelnica" (literally: "Firing Range"). It was intended for POWs from camps located in the occupied territory of Wartheland (Poznania). After modifications, it could have housed as many as 1,500 prisoners.

8 In every case the surnames were spelled phonetically in the original English but have been spelled correctly here. Jarosław Rostkowski (http://stallag-wollstein. bo.pl), a researcher of the camp's history, provided correct spellings of the proper names. Gontarski was the camp commandant after the entry of the Soviets.

9 Modern-day Blachownia Śląska, a district of the city of Kędzierzyn-Koźle in Opole Province (Poland).

10 2nd Lt. Francis R. Clark was the crew navigator on a B-24G Liberator, serial no. 42-78352, pilot: Lt. George Gaines. The aircraft was part of the 15th Air Force, 465th Bomber Group, 781st Squadron. The plane was hit by AAA fire above its objective, which immobilized three engines and caused the fourth one to become engulfed by flames. The pilot attempted to reach the Soviet lines. When this became impossible, the nine crewmen parachuted out. Seven were captured by the Germans and two hidden by the Poles. The side gunner, Sergeant Chapin, was wounded in the arm and remained on the floor of the plane, while Clark was wounded in the leg while attempting a parachute landing.

11 According to information contained in a Military Intelligence Service report from November 1945, the Wolsztyn hospital received very ill or seriously wounded

POWs who could not receive the proper care in the limited conditions of the hospital at Oflag 64. See *American Prisoners of War in Germany*, Chapter 22, Bibliography/XIII.

12 Transit Camp Odessa was opened on February 26, 1945 in the Ukrainian port city for former American POWs and air crews forced to land behind the Soviet lines. On the same day, a transport of American ex-POWs arrived. The 4,600 persons evacuated through TCO had been held mostly at POW camps taken by the Soviets in January and February 1945: Oflag 64 Schubin (Szubin, Kujavia-Pomerania Province), Stalag III-C Alt-Drewitz-Küstrin (Kostrzyn, Lubuskie Province), and Stalag II-B Hammerstein/Schlochau (Czarne, Pomeranian Province). Initially, the Americans wanted the POWs evacuated via Lublin and, afterward, via the still functioning American airbase in Poltava in the Soviet Ukraine, but the last word belonged to the Soviets who refused to endorse this option. The Soviets concentrated the POWs they captured from the Germans in the Polish cities of Kraków, Łódź, Lublin, and Warsaw (Rembertów). On February 22, 1945, the Soviets began to evacuate them to Odessa by train. From February 27 to March 28, 1945, a U.S. mission headed by Lt. Col. James D. Wilmeth, which was to coordinate the evacuation process, operated in the Polish city of Lublin. Although it functioned only for about a month, it nevertheless revealed the impossibility of cooperating with the Soviets. The main evacuation program via Odessa was completed on March 27, 1945 (the evacuations took place on March 7, 15, and 27). Smaller groups, which usually consisted of several or a dozen or so ex-POWs, were evacuated later using either merchant ships or via evacuations of former captives of other nationalities (e.g., on April 7, 18, and 21). Individuals were also evacuated from the USSR via the American Military Mission in Moscow or Poltava. See Defense POW/Missing Personnel Office Washington D.C., U.S.A., Chapter 22, Bibliography/XIII.

13 Following the entry of the Soviets, there were 27 Americans in the area of the camp. Left to their own devices, the ex-POWs initially remained in place. Later, some of them, on their own initiative, journeyed eastward in small groups.

14 The witnesses appended this testimony by stating that the culprits served in SS units. This impression probably resulted from the confusion of the black uniforms worn by Wehrmacht panzer troops, which included skulls on their collar flaps (the insignia of the panzer arm), with SS uniforms. An information report of the Polish insurgent "Kampinos" Group, dated September 17, 1944, described the enemy deployment in the area as follows: "Dziekanów Polski: one company of SS infantry, about 40 vehicles, [and] camouflaged guns in the center of the village. At the end of the village [there are] 3 anti-aircraft guns. ... Dziekanów Niemiecki: a larger number of troops, 14 75 mm and 122 mm guns. Sadowa: no enemy [units]. ... Kiełpin: a labor battalion, and an almost completed bridge. ... Łomianki: a lot of Germans and Hungarians. ... guns by the road, an armored vehicle; Dąbrowa: three companies of Hungarians, a few light guns, supply column, entrenched Germans and Ukrainians, more cannons." Source: Jerzy

Koszada, *"Grupa Kampinos" Partyzanckie Zgrupowanie Armii Krajowej walczące w Powstaniu Warszawskim* [The "Kampinos Group": A Home Army Partisan Unit Fighting in the Warsaw Uprising] (Warsaw: ARS Print Production, 1998), 69. Eyewitness testimonies state that the *Volksdeutsche* inhabiting the village during the war had left. At the time, the only two categories in the locality were either German soldiers or random civilian refugees from Warsaw or the frontline area of Jabłonna–Legionowo. The above data is supplemented by an earlier report by the commander of "Kampinos" Group, Maj. Alfons Kotowski *nom de guerre* "Okoń" from September 13, 1944: "In the area of Czosnów, Kaliszki, Palmiry, Dziekanów, [and] Łomianki are the rear echelons of the SS panzer division 'Wiking.'" Source: *Armia Krajowa w dokumentach 1939–1945. Lipiec–październik 1944, Studium Polski Podziemnej: Londyn,* 319.

15 Statement of September 28, 1945 on a German Crime. Photo copy collection–II 344, IPN, KŚZPNP, BUiAD, Warsaw. The quality of the reproduced document was rather poor and the handwriting sometimes illegible, which required the author to fill in the assumed meaning in brackets.

16 The area of the modern-day Asnyka and Miła (no. 40) Streets.

17 Testimony given in the author's presence in 2004. Compare with Table (Appendix no. 42, p. 185): Polish Red Cross Exhumation Reports–description (distinguishing marks/deposit/comments), and with the testimonies of other witnesses.

18 The road watchman's house exists to this day and is located on Graniczka Street no. 214. The field in question is located by the fork between modern-day Graniczka and Wiklinowa Streets.

19 Currently M. Konopnickiej Street no. 30.

20 The area at the intersection of Warszawska and Ogrodowa Streets near the property at Warszawska Street no. 384.

21 Currently Rolnicza Street no. 206 in the area of Cienista Street which runs in the rear of this property.

22 Now Rolnicza Street no. 212. The labor battalion was building a temporary river crossing in Młociny and, upon its completion, a wooden bridge in Dziekanów Polski.

23 Testimony given in the author's presence in 2004.

24 The properties were owned by the following families at the time: Kłódkiewicz, Rolnicza 214/Piotrowski, Rolnicza 212/Szcześniak, Rolnicza 210/Królak, Rolnicza 208/Bączek, Rolnicza 206.

25 This was the seat of the pilot, Lt. Akins.

26 Currently Asnyka Street.

27 If shot down, the surviving airmen were to attempt to reach the locality of Wiersze (American documents give the coordinates of 52 19 N, 20 39 E as the objective), the headquarters of the Home Army's "Kampinos" Group partisans. The designated password was "Ameryka" [America] and the agreed-on reply was "Polska" [Poland]. See the order of Maj. Alfons Kotowski "Okoń" from September 13,

1944: "To all individuals who reach our positions or move beyond them, and who call out 'Ameryka,' we are to reply with 'Polska' and immediately take them to the headquarters of the Kampinos Group." See: Jerzy Koszada, "*Grupa Kampinos*," 63.

28 In his order issued on August 31, 1944, Lt. Bolesław Szymkiewicz "Znicz" ("Kampinos" Group) ordered that all information on the location and circumstances of the shooting-down of Allied planes carrying assistance to Warsaw be provided, in addition to the aircraft types, and the fate of the crews. He also ordered that a network of observers be created in the countryside. *Armia Krajowa w dokumentach 1939–1945. Lipiec–październik 1944, Studium Polski Podziemnej: Londyn*, 245, 391.

29 *Dziennik Polski i Dziennik Żołnierza*, no. 224, September 21, 1944.

30 We do not know whether this is an erroneous mention of the fate of Lt. Akins' crew, or a mention of the episode of June 21, 1944 (*Frantic 2*), when an aircraft belonging to the 729th Division of the 452nd Bomber Group was shot-down and seven American airmen rescued by the 34th Home Army Infantry Regiment commanded by Lt. Stefan Wyrzykowski "Zenon."

31 Janusz K. Zawodny, *Uczestnicy i świadkowie powstania warszawskiego. Wywiady* [The Participants and Witnesses of the Warsaw Uprising: Interviews] (Warsaw: IPN, 2004), 242. Unfortunately, none of this is mentioned in Adolf Pilch's book *Partyzanci trzech puszcz* [The Partisans of the Three Forests] (Warsaw: Editions Spotkania, 1992).

32 Statement of September 28, 1945 on a German Crime. Photo copy collection, II 344, IPN—KŚZPNP, BUiAD, Warsaw.

33 RL 5 *Luftwaffenpersonalamt Abschußanerkenntnisse Flak*, 314, p. 217, Bundesarchiv–Militärarchiv Freiburg.

34 Ibid., p. 240.

35 RL 5 *Luftwaffenpersonalamt Abschußanerkenntnisse Flak, 68*, p. 5, Bundesarchiv–Militärarchiv Freiburg.

36 RL 5 *Luftwaffenpersonalamt Abschußanerkenntnisse Flak*, 314, p. 248, Bundesarchiv–Militärarchiv Freiburg.

37 Ibid., p. 233.

38 Publications on the 5th SS Panzer Division Wiking also cite testimonies (which have not been mentioned here) describing the unit's capture of some airdropped supplies in the Jabłonna–Poniatów area.

39 Shiller, "Dziesięciu z Latającej Fortecy," [Ten Airmen from a Flying Fortress] in *Lotnictwo, Aviation International*, no. 14 (July 16–31, 1994), 33. The author was unable to ascertain the exact source of the quote provided in the article.

40 Ibid. In this case the author could not ascertain the source of the quote as well.

41 According to Thomas Stotler's testimony (p. XX), Lt. Akins perished as a result of being struck in the head by a bullet or projectile. The skeletal injuries sustained, and especially the cranial fragmentation, allow us to confirm this version of events as well as the testimony of an eyewitness (p. XX) who peeked inside the wreckage after the crash and saw one of the pilots still occupying his seat.

42 Notes based on eyewitness testimonies contain information that the bodies of all the airmen were found inside the planes or close to the machines. These descriptions are quite general, however, and pertain only to all the airmen as a group, not to individuals.

43 This is confirmed by the much more detailed descriptions generated during the autopsies of the remains by the Americans in Belgium in 1949.

44 Author's correspondence with the Institute of National Memory (IPN) in Poland in 2004.

45 Correspondence with Zentrale Stelle der Landesjustizverwaltungen, Ludwigsburg, from 2004 and 2006.

46 In Germany, killings are subject to a 20-year statute of limitations, which means that the murders in question could not be prosecuted after 1964.

Chapter 7

1 "Alianci nad Warszawą," *Wiadomości Powstańcze Dodatek do Biuletynu Informacyjnego* [Insurgent News: A Supplement for the Information Bulletin], no. 31, September 18, 1944.

2 *Biuletyn Okręgu IV PPS i OWPPS Warszawa–Północ* [The Bulletin of District IV of the Polish Socialist Party and the Warsaw District of the Polish Socialist Party: North Warsaw], no. 46, September 18, 1944.

3 *Sprawa* [The Cause], no. 106, September 18, 1944.

4 *Biuletyn Informacyjny*, no. 87, September 19, 1944.

5 *Barykada Warszawa walczy*, no. 39, September 19, 1944.

6 *Robotnik*, no. 56, September 19, 1944.

7 *Armia Ludowa*, no. 34, September 19, 1944.

8 *Armia Ludowa*, no. 35, September 20, 1944.

9 Maciej J. Kwiatkowski, „ *Tu mówi powstańcza Warszawa"…: Dni powstania w audycjach Polskiego radia i dokumentach niemieckich* ["Insurrectionary Warsaw Here" …: The Warsaw Uprising in the Programming of the Polish Radio and German Documents] (Warsaw: 1994), 493–494.

10 Excerpt from *Rzeczpospolita Polska* [The Polish Republic], ibid.

11 Excerpt from "Demonstracja siły," *Robotniki*, ibid.

12 Ibid.

13 This most likely refers to pemmican tea biscuits which were included in some American K-rations.

14 *Armia Krajowa w dokumentach 1939–1945. Lipiec–październik 1944, Studium Polski Podziemnej–Londyn*, 350.

15 Ibid., 349.

16 Ibid., 365.

17 An area then known as "Boernerowo," currently the area of Kleeberga and Podmiejska Streets.

18 *Armia Krajowa w dokumentach 1939–1945. Lipiec–październik 1944, Studium Polski Podziemnej–Londyn*, 362–363.

19 Jan Tarczyński, *Organizacja zrzutów materiałowych dla Armii Krajowej w wybranych dokumentach SPP* [The Organization of Supply Drops for the Home Army in Selected SPP Documents] (London: Polish Underground Movement Study Trust, 2001), 232. Col. Felicjan Majorkiewicz "Iron," the Deputy Commander of Department III of the Main Command, writes that: "Headquarters is demanding the results of the American airdrop. Two positions emerged in discussions on this subject. Some argued that the number of captured containers should be corrected upward in the hope of receiving other drops consisting of at least 100 containers. Others maintained that Headquarters should be given the factual number of captured containers … Eventually, the inflated numbers were dispatched to London and Headquarters was told that 228 containers had been captured, of which 77 fell in no-man's land. Of these, 45 were captured in combat. In addition, 28 containers were lost as a result of their parachutes being pierced by incendiary bullets from German machine guns." Felicjan Majorkiewicz, *Lata chmurne, lata dumne* [Cloudy Years, Proud Years] (Warsaw: Instytut Wydawniczy PAX, 1983), 291.

20 The matter is quite intriguing because only the lead bombardier of each wing kept track of the chosen bombing course. The other aircraft adhered to their place in the tight formation and followed the lead of the head bomber. Thus, it is difficult to ascertain the exact scale of this error.

21 If the question is at all addressed, the results are assessed as good or very good. See the communiqué of the headquarters of the American strategic air force in Europe.

22 *Dziennik Polski i Dziennik Żołnierza*, no. 223, September 20, 1944.

23 Since this group headed the expedition, it was the first to encounter Flak fire in the area of Modlin–Łomianki.

24 Damaged planes: Tactical Bomber Wing A: 43-38274 R. J. Fackelman and 42-102505 Q. O. Gilbert: aircraft left in Poltava; Wing B: 44-8315 P. R. Hibbard, 42-32026 P. Goodrich, 43-37565 F. G. Galetti: aircraft left in Mirgorod; 42-102677 G. W. Johnston: aircraft left in Brześć Litewski; Wing C: 43-38472 F. F. Danne: aircraft left in Mirgorod.

25 The airmen who remained in Piriatyn were Maj. Emil L. Sluga, Capt. Fred R. Haviland Jr., and Lieutenants Charles H. Spencer, Keo L. Snook, Bradley Watkins, and James Monchan.

26 *USSAFE Warsaw Dropping Operation*, microfilm A 5689. All quotes cited here are excerpts of this document.

27 The time period in question is September 14–22. Some of the aircraft did not return to base until October 7.

28 This fact is mentioned in Lt. Charles C. Nielsen's testimony cited earlier, who recalled a 20-min flight attracting constant Flak fire. See p. XX: "Before the IP we had …."

29 Stanisław Szulczyński, *Organizacja i działania bojowe ludowego Wojska Polskiego w latach 1943–1945* [The Organization and Combat Missions of the People's Polish Military in 1943–1945], Vol. 2 Part 1 (Warsaw: Wydawnictwo MON, 1962), 510–511.

30 Ibid., 586.

31 Józef Margules, *Boje 1 Armii WP w obszarze Warszawy (sierpień–wrzesień 1944)* [The Battles of the 1st Army of the Polish Military in the Warsaw Area: August–September 1944] (Warsaw: Wydawnictwo MON, 1967), 381.

32 Józef Margules, *Przyczółki warszawskie* [Warsaw Bridgeheads] (Warsaw: Wydawnictwo MON, 1962), 302–303.

33 Zenon Kliszko, *Powstanie warszawskie, Artykuły, Przemówienia, Wspomnienia, Dokumenty* [The Warsaw Uprising: Articles, Speeches, Reminiscences, Documents] (Warsaw: KiW, 1967), 269–271.

34 "Powstanie Warszawskie w dokumentach sowieckich" [The Warsaw Uprising in Soviet Documents], *Wojskowy Przegląd Historyczny*, no. 3 (149) (July–September 1994), 239.

35 Józef Margules, *Na oczach Kremla. Tragedia walczącej Warszawy w świetle dokumentów rosyjskich* [In the Plain Sight of the Kremlin: The Tragedy of Fighting Warsaw in Light of Russian Documents] (Warsaw: Agencja Wydawnicza „Egros." Wojskowy Instytut Historyczny, 1994), 226.

36 Pilot: G. W. Johnston; second pilot: M. R. Robinson; bombardier: F. D. O'Neill; navigator: D. L. Lash; radio operator: W. S. Parks; upper turret gunner–mechanic: R. P. Hardy; tail gunner: B. Marshall; lower turret gunner: D. C. Kelly; side gunner: J. S. Lawman; photographer/passenger: L. Cusano.

37 Margules, *Na oczach Kremla*, 226–227.

38 Ibid., 227–228.

39 Ibid., 230.

40 Sabina Sebyłowa, *Notatki z prawobrzeżnej Warszawy* [Notes from Right-Bank Warsaw] (Warsaw: Czytelnik, 1985), 362–363.

41 During the meeting Maj. Gen. Anderson cited information provided by the War Department to President Roosevelt in September 1944: "The cost of these missions in relation to our offensive effort in Western Europe, and the losses which our Air Force could incur while carrying out this project, mean that it would be wise to discontinue any further efforts to airlift supplies for the Poles." Simultaneously, he also addressed the issues behind this decision in his "Memorandum: Warsaw Relief Operations" of October 15, in which he noted that: "The situation [in Warsaw] was becoming so desperate that it would have been inappropriate to stress military effectiveness in the face of such suffering." See *USSAFE Warsaw Dropping Operation*, microfilm A 5689.

42 Scheduled take-off: Zero Hour (ZH), 0730 h; objective to be reached at ZH + 276 minutes (1206 h); supplies to be dropped from an altitude of 14,000 ft; bombers to land at Poltava base at ZH + 473 minutes (1523 h); fighters to land at Piriatyn base.

43 *Armia Krajowa w dokumentach 1939–1945. Lipiec–październik 1944, Studium Polski Podziemnej–Londyn*, 411–412.

44 The surrender agreement was scheduled to go into effect on the same day at 2100 h Warsaw time.

45 The decision was brought to Poltava on September 1 by the commander of Eastern Command, Maj. Gen. Walsh. It was made at Caserta in Italy, where the representatives of the USSTAF approved a provisional winter plan to conduct operations utilizing only the base in Poltava, which was manned by 200–300 people. The matter was quite delicate, however, for the Americans did not wish to convey to the Soviets that they were abandoning the insurgents in Warsaw by beginning their preparations to reduce their Eastern Command personnel.

46 The base in Piriatyn was closed down on September 30, while the first train evacuating American personnel departed Mirgorod on October 7.

47 *Dziennik Personalny nr 4 z dnia 29.09.1944* [Personal Diary No. 4 of September 29, 1944] (London: SPP).

48 *Wings: Periodical of the Polish Air Force*, no. 19/445, October 15, 1944.

Chapter 8

1 John T. Correll, "The Poltava Debacle," *Air Force Magazine* 94, no. 3 (March 2011), accessed at http://www.airforcemag.com/MagazineArchive/Pages/2011/March%202011/0311Poltava.aspx

2 It should be emphasized that rumors that the Soviets treated American dead with disrespect cannot be confirmed, but according to Lane, it was accepted by the American air attaché in Poland, Lt. Col. Edward York. York participated in the Doolittle raid and was interned in the Soviet Union for 14 months. See Arthur Bliss Lane, *I Saw Poland Betrayed* (New York: Bobbs-Merrill, 1948), 31–33. On York, see http://www.co.genesee.ny.us/departments/history/edward_joseph_%28cichowski%29_york.html

Appendix 2

1 *Życie Warszawy*, no. 222, 17 September 1984.

2 *Życie Warszawy*, no. 223, 18 September 1984. A similar announcement was also printed in Express Wieczorny, no. 186, 19 September 1984.

3 *Pismo przewodniczącego Zespół ds. Nadania Nazw Osiedlom, Placom i Ulicom w Warszawie z dnia 17.07.87* [The letter of the head of the Unit for the Purpose of Naming Residential Complexes, Squares, and Streets in Warsaw], L.dz. BRNVIII/014/171/87. The letter was written in response to Ryszard Szcześniak's request.

Bibliography

Published books and articles

Aders, G. and Werner, H. (1999) *Jadgeschwader 51 "Mölders" Eine Chronik Berichte, Erlebnisse, Dokumente*. Stuttgart, Motorbuch.

Armia Krajowa w dokumentach 1939–1945. Lipiec–październik 1944, Studium Polski Podziemnej: Londyn [The Home Army in Documents, 1939–1945. July–October 1944, A Study of Underground Poland: London], Vol. IV. Wrocław: Zakład Narodowy im. Ossolińskich, Wydawnictwo, 1991.

(2006) *B-17 Bomber: Pilot's Flight Operating Instructions*. Los Angeles: Periscope Film, reprint of 1942.

Baker, I. C. (1945) *Reference Manual for Personal Equipment Officers*. N.p.: George A. Peterson, n.d; reprint of Jan. 1945.

Bartelski, L. M. (2004) *Mokotów, Warszawskie Termopile 1944* [Mokotów: Warsaw's Thermopylae, 1944]. Warsaw, Fundacja "Warszawa walczy 1939–1945".

Bielecki, R. (1994) *W zasięgu PAST-y* [Within Reach of PAST]. Warsaw, Czytelnik.

Bieniecki, K. (1994) *Lotnicze Wsparcie Armii Krajowej* [Supporting the Home Army by Air]. Kraków, Arcana.

Bojemski, S. (2002) *Poszli w Skier Powodzi: Narodowe Siły Zbrojne w Powstaniu Warszawskim*. Warsaw, Glaukopis.

Brym-Zdunin, Z. (1992) *Żelazna Reduta* [The Iron Redoubt]. London, Polska Fundcja Kulturalna.

Churchill, W. S. (1950) *The Second World War*. Vol. 6: *Triumph and Tragedy*. New York, Houghton Mifflin.

Ciechanowski, J. M. (1992) *Na Tropach Tragedii. Powstanie Warszawskie 1944* [On the Road to Tragedy: The Warsaw Uprising of 1944]. Warsaw, Polska Oficyna Wydawnicza "BGW".

Conversino, M. J. (1997) *Fighting with the Soviets: The Failure of Operation FRANTIC 1944–1945*. Lawrence, University Press of Kansas.

Davies, N. (2005) *Rising '44: The Battle for Warsaw.* New York, Penguin.

Dziennik związkowy [The Union Daily], Chicago, 12–14 June 1992.

Garliński, J. (1971) *Politycy i żołnierze* [Politicians and Soldiers]. London, Odnova Ltd.

Haney, S. L. (1994) "Postal History: Personal and Poignant. 1944 Uprising" in *The American Philatelist.* September 1944.

Infield, G. B. (1973) *The Poltava Affair: A Russian Warning, an American Tragedy.* New York, Macmillan.

Jewsienicki, W. (1989) *Powstanie Warszawskie 1944 Okiem Polskiej Kamery* [The Warsaw Uprising through the Lenses of Polish Cameras]. Warsaw, Interpress.

Kledzik, M. (1984) *Królewska 16* [Królewska Street no. 16]. Warsaw, Instytut Wydawniczy PAX.

―――. (1994) *IV Zgrupowanie AK "Gurt" w Powstaniu Warszawskim, Między Marszałkowską i Żelazną Al. Sikorskiego i Pańską* [The Fourth Home Army Group "Gurt" in the Warsaw Uprising: Between Marszałkowska, Żelazna, Sikorskiego, and Pańska Streets]. Warsaw, BICOP Sp. z o.o.

Kliszko, Z. (1967) *Powstanie warszawskie, Artykuły, Przemówienia, Wspomnienia, Dokumenty* [The Warsaw Uprising: Articles, Speeches, Reminiscences, and Documents]. Warsaw, KiW.

Komorowski, T. (1979) *Armia Podziemna* [The Underground Army]. London, SPP.

Koszada, J.(1998) *"Grupa Kampinos" Partyzanckie Zgrupowanie Armii Krajowej walczące w Powstaniu Warszawskim* [The "Kampinos Group": The Home Army Partisan Grouping Fighting in the Warsaw Uprising]. Warsaw, ARS Print Production.

Kwiatkowski, M. J. (1994) *"Tu mówi powstańcza Warszawa"..., Dni Powstania w audycjach Polskiego radia i dokumentach niemieckich* ["This is Insurgent Warsaw": The Days of the Uprising in Polish Radio Programming and German Documents]. Warsaw, Biblioteka Syrenki.

Lane, A. B. (1948) *I Saw Poland Betrayed.* New York, Bobbs-Merrill.

Leciński, R. ed., (1960) *Korespondencja Przewodniczącego Rady Ministrów ZSRR z prezydentem Stanów Zjednoczonych i premierem Wielkiej Brytanii w okresie Wielkiej Wojny Narodowej 1941–1945* [The Correspondence of the Head of the Soviet Council of Ministers with the President of the United States and the Prime Minister of Great Britain during the Great Patriotic War, 1941–1945], vols. 1–2. Warsaw, Wydawnictwo MON.

Lopez, P. (2004) "Hero in a far-off land" in *Star Tribune: Newspaper of the Twin Cities,* 23 June 2004.

Lukas, R. C. "Marcus Shook: A Mississippi Hero," *Mississippi History Now,* online, http://www.mshistorynow.mdah.ms.gov/articles/407/marcus-shook-a-mississippi-hero (accessed Sept. 2, 2017).

Majorkiewicz, F. (1983) *Lata chmurne, lata dumne* [Cloudy Years, Proud Days]. Warsaw, Instytut Wydawniczy PAX.

Malinowski, K. (1983) *Żołnierze łączności walczącej Warszawy* [Fighting Warsaw's Communications Troops]. Warsaw, Instytut Wydawniczy PAX.

Margules, J. (1962) *Przyczółki warszawskie* [The Warsaw Bridgeheads]. Warsaw, Wydawnictwo MON.

———. (1967) *Boje 1 Armii WP w obszarze Warszawy. sierpień–wrzesień 1944* [The Battles of the 1st Army of the Polish Military in the Warsaw Area, August–September 1944]. Warsaw, Wydawnictwo MON.

———. (1994) *Na oczach Kremla. Tragedia walczącej Warszawy w świetle dokumentów rosyjskich* [Before the Kremlin's Very Eyes: The Tragedy of Fighting Warsaw in Light of Russian Documents]. Warsaw, Agencja Wydawnicza "Egros" Wojskowy Instytut Historyczny.

Marshall, W. (1984) *Angels, Bulldogs and Dragons: The 355th Fighter Group in World War II*. Mesa, AZ, Campion Fighter Museum.

Matecki, J. (1969) "Dziennik działań niemieckiej 9 Armii" [The Report Book of the German 9th Army] in *Zeszyty Historyczne*, no. 15. Paris, Instytut Literacki.

"Na Przedpolu Warszawy," http://www.ibprs.pl/ak_obroza_kampinos/43.html

Nowicki, J. (1991) "Boeing B-17 Flying Fortress," *Militaria Lotnicze*, No. 1. Warsaw.

Organizacja i działania bojowe ludowego Wojska Polskiego [The Organization and Combat Operations of the Polish People's Military], vols. 1–4. Warsaw, Wydawnictwo MON. 1958–1965.

Orpen, N. (1984) *Airlift to Warsaw: The Rising of 1944*. Norman, University of Oklahoma Press.

Piekarski, M. (1980) "Do zobaczenia" [I'll Be Seeing You], *Stolica*, no. 37/38, Warsaw.

Polskie Siły Zbrojne w Drugiej Wojnie Światowej [The Polish Armed Forces during the Second World War], vol. III, *Armia Krajowa* [The Home Army]. London, Instytut Historyczny im. Gen. Sikorskiego, 1950.

Przemyski, P. A. (1991) *Z pomocą żołnierzom podziemia* [Assisting the Underground Soldiers]. Warsaw: WKŁ.

Sawicki, T. (2001) *Rozkaz: zdławić powstanie* [The Order to Snuff Out the Uprising]. Warsaw, Dom Wydawniczy Bellona.

Sebyłowa, S. (1985) *Notatki z prawobrzeżnej Warszawy* [Notes from Right-Bank Warsaw]. Warsaw, Czytelnik.

Shiller, J. (1994) "Dziesięciu z Latającej Fortecy" [Ten Airmen from a Flying Fortress] in *Lotnictwo, Aviation International*, no. 14, 16–31 July 1994.

Slessor, J. (1956) *The Central Blue: Recollections and Reflections*. London, Cassell and Company Limited.

Szcześniak, J. (2009) "Operation Carpetbagger" in *Lotnictwo*, no. 1/2.

Szpilman, W. (2000) *The Pianist: The Extraordinary True Story of One Man's Survival in Warsaw, 1939–1945*. New York, Picador.

Tarczyński, J. (2001) *Organizacja zrzutów materiałowych dla Armii Krajowej w wybranych dokumentach* [The Organization of Airdrops for the Home Army in Selected Documents]. London, SPP.

(1985) *The 390th Veterans Association/Foundation Newsletter*, vol. 1, no. 3, Tucson, Arizona.

(1987) *The 390th Veterans Association / Foundation Newsletter*, vol. 3, no. 1, Tucson, Arizona.

Utracka, K. (2002) *Zgrupowanie AK Chrobry II* [The Chrobry II Grouping of the Home Army]. Warsaw, Dom Wydawniczy Bellona.

Wells, K. (1996) *Steeple Morden Strafers, 1943–45: The Unit History of the 355th Fighter Group of the 8th Air Force.* Steeple Morden, Cambridgeshire, Egon.

(1994) "Powstanie Warszawskie w dokumentach sowieckich" [The Warsaw Uprising in Soviet Documents] in *Wojskowy Przegląd Historyczny*, no. 3. 149, July–September. Warsaw, Wojskowy Instytut Historyczny.

Zabiełło, S. (1957) "Pomoc Anglosasów dla Powstania Warszawskiego" [Anglo-Saxon Assistance for the Warsaw Uprising] in *Najnowsze dzieje Polski 1939–1945* [Poland's Most Recent History, 1939–1945], vol. 1. Warsaw, PWN.

Zagórski, W. (1990) [Lech Grzybowski], *Wicher wolności, Dziennik powstańca* [The Wind of Freedom: An Insurgent's Diary]. Warsaw, Czytelnik.

Zaremba, Z. (1957) *Wojna i konspiracja* [War and Underground Activity]. London, B. Świderski.

Zawodny, J. K. (1978) *Nothing but Honour: The Story of the Warsaw Uprising 1944.* Stanford, CA, Hoover Institution Press.

———. (1994) *Powstanie warszawskie w walce i dyplomacji* [The Warsaw Uprising in Diplomacy and Combat]. Warsaw, Wydawnictwo Naukowe PWN.

———. (2004) *Uczestnicy i świadkowie Powstania Warszawskiego. Wywiady* [The Eyewitnesses and Participants of the Warsaw Uprising: Interviews]. Warsaw, IPN.

Żenczykowski, T. (1985) *Samotny bój Warszawy* [Warsaw's Lonely Fight]. Paris, Editions Spotkania.

Archival sources

Archiwum Akt Nowych [The Archive of New Records], Warsaw, Poland

Alexandria Microfiche:

Armeeoberkomando 9/19.09.1944/ 7.20 Uhr/An Oberkomando Heeresgruppe Mitte [Army High Command to the High Command of Army Group Center, September 19, 1944, 0720 hours] / I a Nr. T 13036/44 tjn.

Oberkommando der Heeresgruppe Mitte Tagesmeldung [Daily Report of the High Command of Army Group Center] 18.09.1944/19.09.1944/00.15 Uhr/I a Nr. T 4848/44 tjn.

Oberkommando der Heeresgruppe Mitte Tagesmeldung [Daily Report of the High Command of Army Group Center] 19.09.1944/20.09.44/1.00 Uhr/I a Nr. T 4864/44 tjn.

Kriegstagebuch Nr. 11 der Führungsabteilung Textband [Daily War Log no. 11 of the Command Unit] 1. Ausfertigung Berichtszwit 11.07.44 – 31.12.44. AOK 9.

The National Library, Warsaw, Poland

Express Wieczorny [Evening Express], no. 169, November 7, 1946.
Kurier Codzienny [Daily Courier], no. 236. 409, November 7, 1946.
Życie Warszawy [Warsaw Life], no. 306. 735, November 7, 1946.

The Archive of the Polish Underground: 1939–1956, Warsaw

Armia Ludowa [People's Army], no. 34, September 19, 1944.
Armia Ludowa, no. 35, September 20, 1944.
Barykada Warszawa Walczy [The Barricade: Fighting Warsaw], no. 38, September 19, 1944.
Barykada Warszawa walczy, no. 39, September 19, 1944.
Barykada Wolności, organ Robotniczej Partii Polskich Socjalistów [Barricade of Freedom: The Publication of the Workers' Party of Polish Socialists], no. 148, September 21, 1944.
Biuletyn Informacyjny [Information Bulletin], no. 87, September 19, 1944.
Biuletyn Informacyjny, no. 88, September 20, 1944.
Biuletyn Krajowy [National Bulletin], no. 72, September 18, 1944.
Biuletyn Okręgu IV PPS i OWPPS Warszawa-Północ [Bulletin of District IV of the Polish Socialist Party and the PPS Warsaw District, Warsaw-North], no. 46, September 18, 1944.
Biuletyn wiadomości [News Bulletin], no. 95, September 18, 1944.
Biuletyn wiadomości, no. 97, September 19, 1944.
Dziennik Polski i Dziennik Żołnierza [The Polish Daily and the Soldier's Daily], no. 223, September 20, 1944.
Dziennik Polski i Dziennik Żołnierza, no. 224, September 21, 1944.
Dziennik Polski i Dziennik Żołnierza, no. 226, September 23, 1944.
Komunikat powstańczej Polskiej Agencji Telegraficznej [Communique of the Insurgent Polish Telegraph Agency], September 18, 1944.
Nowy Kurier Warszawski [New Warsaw Courier], no. 224, September 24, 1944.
Robotnik, Centralny organ PPS [The Worker: The Central Publication of the Polish Socialist Party], no. 56, September 19, 1944.
Sprawa [The Cause], no. 106, September 18, 1944.
Wiadomości Powstańcze, Dodatek do Biuletynu Informacyjnego [Insurgent News: An Addendnum to the Information Bulletin], no. 31, September 18, 1944.
Wings, Periodical of the Polish Air Force, no. 19/445, October 15, 1944.

390th Bomb Group Memorial Museum, Tucson

Combat Mission Report, no. 191, September 18, 1944/September 23, 1944.
Operations Narrative of Mission no. 191, September 18, 1944/September 24, 1944.
Roster of Mission no. 191, 390th Group, September 18, 1944/September 24, 1944.

Bundesarchiv-Militärarchiv [Federal/Military Archive], Freiburg

"Der Einsatz der Luftflotte 6 im Rahmen des Kampfes um Warschau [The Task of the 6th Air Fleet in the Battle for Warsaw] vom 1.8.–2.10.1944," RL 7/554

"Luftwaffenpersonalamt Abschu⊠anerkenntnisse Flak," RL 5; RL 5/68 pp. 1–10; RL 5/168 pp. 103–123; and RL 5/314 pp. 208–280.

Department of the Air Force, Air Force Historical Research Agency, Maxwell Air Force Base

8 AF Mission Reports, microfilm A 5993.

3rd Bomb Division Mission Reports, microfilm B 5482.

355th Fighter Group, microfilm B 0313.

Missing Air Crew Report 10205/Individual Casualty Questionnaire/Casualty Questionnaire.

Missing Air Crew Report 9238.

Missing Air Crew Report 9239.

Missing Air Crew Report 9010.

USSAFE Warsaw Dropping Operation, microfilm A 5689.

Department of the Army, U.S. Total Army Human Resources Command, Alexandria

Individual Deceased Personnel File: Francis E. Akins.

Individual Deceased Personnel File: Clyde A. Arrants.

Individual Deceased Personnel File: Ely Berenson.

Individual Deceased Personnel File: Frank P. De Cillis.

Individual Deceased Personnel File: Paul F. Haney.

Individual Deceased Personnel File: Paul R. Hibbard.

Individual Deceased Personnel File: George A. Mac Phee.

Individual Deceased Personnel File: Myron S. Merrill.

Individual Deceased Personnel File: Robert O. Peters.

Individual Deceased Personnel File: Walter P. Shimshock.

Individual Deceased Personnel File: Forrest D. Show.

Individual Deceased Personnel File: Joseph J. Vigna.

Other U.S. Military records

American Prisoners of War in Germany, Prepared by Military Intelligence Service War Department, OFLAG 64. accessed in November 2006, www.rlc.dcccd.edu/enrich/cordstud/prsonr64.htm

Riddling, Jan, Cindy Goodman, and Ted Chodorowski. "The Uprising," Defense POW, Missing Personnel Office Washington, D.C., accessed in November 2006, www.dtic.mil/dpmo

Instytut Pamięci Narodowej [Institute of National Memory], Warsaw

Protokół z dnia 28 września 1945 r o zbrodni niemieckiej. Zbiór fotokopii [Report from September 28, 1945 on a German Crime, Photocopy collection]–II 344, IPN–KŚZPNP, BUiAD in Warsaw.

Polish Red Cross, Warsaw

Oświadczenie dotyczące depozytu: załącznik do protokółu [Statement on Deposited Items: Addendum] no. 245, PCK Okręg Warszawski [Warsaw Chapter of the Polish Red Cross], November 8, 1946.

Protokół dotyczący pochówku we wsi Kątne. PCK Delegatura Oddziałowa w Nasielsku [Protocol on the burial in Kątne village, the Polish Red Cross District Plenipotentiary in Nasielsk], November 27, 1946.

Protokóły ekshumacyjne: nr od 242 do 249, PCK Okręg Warszawski [Exhumation Protocols: nos. 242–249, Warsaw District of the Polish Red Cross], November 5, 1946.

Studium Polski Podziemnej [The Study of Underground Poland], London

Dziennik Personalny nr 4 z dnia [Personal Daily Log of] 29.09.1944, London, SPP.

Unpublished manuscripts and testimonies

Francis R. Clark, "Five combat missions; then fifty more."

Bob Gillmore, "Recollections from the Third Mission to Russia in WWII," February 11, 2004

Bert W. Marshall, "September 18: account."

Jerzy Shiller, "Uwagi na temat zdjęć ze zrzutu lotnictwa U.S.A. 18 IX 1944 w rejonie Warszawy" [Comments on the Photographs of the US Air Force Airdrop in the Warsaw Area on September 18, 1944], Los Angeles, March 1981, SPP.

Personal collection Jerzy Szcześniak

Express Wieczorny [Evening Express], no. 186, September 19, 1984.

Map–Warschau. [Warsaw] Nord [North], scale: 1:100 000 Grossblatt no. 357, 1940, German reproduction of a prewar Polish WIG map.

Pismo przewodniczącego Zespół ds. Nadania Nazw Osiedlom, Placom i Ulicom w Warszawie z dnia 17.07.87 [Letter from the Head of the Section to Name Residential Complexes, Squares, and Streets in Warsaw from July 17,1987] L.dz. BRNVIII/014/171/87.

Życie Warszawy [Warsaw Life], no. 222, September 17, 1984.

Życie Warszawy, no. 223, September 18, 1984.

Internet sources

Website of the 100th Bomber Group, accessed in November 2006, www.100thbg.com

"Operation Titanic [Frantic]" U.S. War Department film, Army Pictoral Service Signal Corps, 1944. Accessed online: https://www.youtube.com/watch?v=RrkKV2KTZ50 (Sept. 2, 2017).

Testimonies and diaries

Sergeant Bill J. Bates, side gunner, 349th Bomber Squadron.

Maj. Marvin S. "Red" Bowman, intelligence officer, 100th Bomber Group.

Lt. Grant A. Fuller, co-pilot, 418th Bomber Squadron.

Lt. Rowland L. Hetrick, navigator, 350th Bomber Squadron.

Lt. Art H. Juhlin, navigator, 418th Bomber Squadron.

Senior Sergeant Glenn Smiley, radio operator, 350th Bomber Squadron.

Sergeant James H. Smith, Jr., side gunner, 351st Bomber Squadron.

Skarbek-Kruszewski, Zygmunt. "Bellum Vobiscum War Memoirs," accessed in September 2017, www.skarbek.com.au/bv/

http://stalag-wollstein.bo.pl. accessed in January 2011.

Oral recollection (noted or recorded), and letters or email testimonies

Carolyn Beaubien, Jerzy Boć, Klemens Bogurat, Francis R. Clark, Willis S. Cole Jr. "Sam," Jack Culbertson, Edward Figauzer, Tim Foppiano, Steve Gotts, Suzanne L. Haney, Franciszka Kłódkiewicz, Elżbieta Królak, Norman Malayney, Janina Niegodzisz, Stanisław Pasternak, Garnett L. Akins Rainey, Peter Randall, Jarosław Rostkowski, Fred Sachs, A. Berkley Sanborn, Jerzy Shiller, Marcus L. Shook, Jerzy Sienkiewicz, Józef Sopiński, Vincent J. Stefanek, Krzysztof Stoliński, Wojciech Szabłowski, Stefan Szcześniak, Bernard Szymczak, Ken Wells, and Ryszard Wiśniewski.